The Peter Principle

The Peter Principle

by *Laurence J. Peter*

&

RAYMOND HULL

William Morrow & Company, INC.

NEW YORK · 1969

Library of Congress Cataloging
in Publication Data
ISBN 0-688-02289-8
ISBN 0-688-27544-3 pbk.

Printed in the United States of America.

22   23   24   25

This book is dedicated to all those who,
working, playing, loving, living and
dying at their Level of Incompetence,
provided the data for the founding and
development of the salutary science of
Hierarchiology.

They saved others: themselves they could not save.

Foreword

by LAURENCE J. PETER

It is sometimes difficult for the discoverer of a principle to identify accurately that moment when the revelation occurred. The Peter Principle did not enter my consciousness in a flash of recognition, but I became aware of it gradually over several years of observation of man's incompetence. It therefore seems appropriate I should present the reader with a historical account of my discovery.

A Clot for Every Slot

Although some people function competently, I observed others who had risen above their level of competence and were habitually bungling their jobs, frustrating their co-workers and eroding the efficiency of the organization. It was logical to conclude that for every job that existed in the world there was someone, somewhere, who could not do it. Given sufficient time and enough promotions he would get that job!

I was not concerned with the oversight, the slip of the tongue, the faux pas, the occasional error which can be an embarrassment to any of us. Anyone can make a mistake. The most competent men throughout history have had their lapses. Conversely, the habitually incompetent can, by random action, be right once in a while. Instead, I was searching for the underlying principle which would explain why so many important positions were occupied by persons incompetent to fulfill the duties and responsibilities of their respective offices.

Rot at the Top

The first public presentation of the Peter Principle occurred at a seminar in September, 1960, when I addressed a group of directors of federally funded educational research projects. Because each participant had written a successful grant proposal, each had been rewarded by a promotion to a position as director of one or more research projects. Some of these men actually had research skills, but this was irrelevant to their acquiring the directorship. Many others were inept at research design and, in desperation, were simply intending to replicate some oft-repeated statistical exercise.

As I became aware of their plan to spend time and taxpayers' money on rediscovering the wheel, I decided to explain their predicament by introducing them to the Peter Principle. Their reaction to my presentation was a mixture of hostility and laughter. A young statistician in the group convulsed with laughter and literally fell from his chair. Later he confided that his intense reaction was caused by my humorous presentation of outrageous ideas while at the same time he was watching the district research director's face turn red, then purple.

Tongue in Both Cheeks

Although case studies were accurately compiled and data realistic, I had decided to present the Peter Principle exclusively in satirical form. Therefore, in all lectures from 1960 to 1964, and in the articles that followed, examples with a humorous connotation were used and fictitious names were employed to protect the guilty.

All Rights Reserved

It was in December, 1963, during the intermission of a badly presented play that I explained to Raymond Hull why the actor playing the lead was saying his lines with his back to the audience and gesturing into the wings. This formerly competent actor had found his level of incompetence by attempting to be a combination actor-director-producer. In the conversation that ensued, Mr. Hull convinced me that I was not doing justice to the Peter Principle by presenting it to only a select few who might attend my lectures. He insisted that it should be available to the world in book form. He further suggested that without publication and copyright, someone else might attach his name to my discovery. A collaboration was agreed upon and the manuscript was completed in the spring of 1965.

Victims of the Peter Principle

The final manuscript was submitted to the editors of a number of major publishing houses. The first returned it with an accompanying letter which stated: "We can see no commercial possibilities for this work and cannot encourage you to continue with it. Even with interdivisional sales the publication of this work is not warranted." The next editor wrote: "You should not deal so lightly with such a serious topic." Another suggested: "If you are writing a comedy, it should not contain so many tragic case studies." Still another said: "I will reconsider publication if you will make up your mind and rewrite this as a humorous book or as a serious scientific work." Fourteen rejection notices and two years later I began to doubt whether the world was ready for my discovery.

A Bit at a Time

It was decided that if the publishing world was not ready for a book then perhaps we might introduce the Peter Principle gradually through several short articles. Mr. Hull completed an article for *Esquire* magazine for December, 1966. Later I wrote about the principle for West Magazine (*Los Angeles Times*, April 17, 1967). The response to this article was overwhelming. Over four hundred letters were received within a few months. Requests for lectures and articles poured in and as many as possible were fulfilled.

The Selling of the Principle, 1968

In March, 1968, the President of William Morrow inquired about the possibility of a book about the Peter Principle. I dusted off the manuscript and handed it to a William Morrow editor.

The book, released in February, 1969, gradually climbed to the number one position on the nonfiction best-seller list where it stayed for twenty weeks. It remained on the best-seller list for over a year and has now been translated into fourteen languages. The book has been required reading in a number of university courses and has been the subject of discussion for many seminars.

The book has also inspired several serious research projects investigating the validity of the principle. Each research supports the correctness of my observations.

Quit While You Are Behind

Since publication of the book I have had many opportunities to reach my own level of incompetence in one giant step. I have declined many offers to become a management consultant and to conduct seminars for business administrators. Although these proposals were rejected I have not been protected from the Peter Principle. Recently a school of business administration invited me to give a lecture and then scheduled my appearance in no less than five different rooms at the same time. An association of industrial engineers and systems experts asked me to address their convention but misinformed me regarding the date, the time, and the place. Appliances I have purchased still fail to operate, or break down within thirty days, my car is returned from the service shop with mysterious defects, and the government continues to increase the number of regulations which influence my life, while it ensnares itself in bureaucratic red tape.

Death Is Nature's Warning to Slow Down

As individuals we tend to climb to our levels of incompetence. We behave as though *up* is better and *more* is better, and yet all around us we see the tragic victims of this mindless escalation.

We see men in groups, and most of the human race, struggling for status on a treadmill to oblivion, escalating warfare and weaponry to overkill the population of the world, escalating production of power and products while polluting the environment and upsetting the life-supporting ecological balance.

If man is going to rescue himself from a future intolerable existence, he must first see where his unmindful escalation is leading him. He must examine his objectives and see that true progress is achieved through moving *forward* to a better way of life, rather than *upward* to total life incompetence. Man must realize that improvement of the quality of experience is more important than the acquisition of useless artifacts and material possessions. He must reassess the meaning of life and decide whether he will use his intellect and technology for the preservation of the human race and the development of the humanistic characteristics of man, or whether he will continue to utilize his creative potential in escalating a super-collosal deathtrap.

Man, on occasion, has caught a glimpse of his reflection in a mirror, and not immediately recognizing himself, has begun to laugh before realizing what he was doing. It is in such moments that true progress toward understanding has occurred. This book is intended to be that mirror.

Laurence J. Peter
August, 1970.

Contents

The Peter Principle

Introduction

by RAYMOND HULL

As an author and journalist, I have had exceptional opportunities to study the workings of civilized society. I have investigated and written about government, industry, business, education and the arts. I have talked to, and listened carefully to, members of many trades and professions, people of lofty, middling and lowly stations.

I have noticed that, with few exceptions, men bungle their affairs. Everywhere I see incompetence rampant, incompetence triumphant.

I have seen a three-quarter-mile-long highway bridge collapse and fall into the sea because, despite checks and double-checks, someone had botched the design of a supporting pier.

I have seen town planners supervising the development of a city on the flood plain of a great river, where it is certain to be periodically inundated.

Lately I read about the collapse of three giant cooling towers at a British power-station: they cost a million dollars each, but were not strong enough to withstand a good blow of wind.

I noted with interest that the indoor baseball stadium at Houston, Texas, was found on completion to be peculiarly ill-suited to baseball: on bright days, fielders could not see fly balls against the glare of the skylights.

I observe that appliance manufacturers, as regular policy,

9

establish regional service depots in the expectation—justified by experience—that many of their machines will break down during the warranty period.

Having listened to umpteen motorists' complaints about faults in their new cars, I was not surprised to learn that roughly one-fifth of the automobiles produced by major manufacturers in recent years have been found to contain potentially dangerous production defects.

Please do not assume that I am a jaundiced ultra-conservative, crying down contemporary men and things just because they are contemporary. Incompetence knows no barriers of time or place.

Macaulay gives a picture, drawn from a report by Samuel Pepys, of the British navy in 1684. "The naval administration was a prodigy of wastefulness, corruption, ignorance, and indolence . . . no estimate could be trusted . . . no

In the expectation that many of their machines will break down during the warranty period.

contract was performed . . . no check was enforced. . . . Some of the new men of war were so rotten that, unless speedily repaired, they would go down at their moorings. The sailors were paid with so little punctuality that they were glad to find some usurer who would purchase their tickets at forty percent discount. Most of the ships which were afloat were commanded by men who had not been bred to the sea."

Wellington, examining the roster of officers assigned to him for the 1810 campaign in Portugal, said, "I only hope that when the enemy reads the list of their names, he trembles as I do."

Civil War General Richard Taylor, speaking of the Battle of the Seven Days, remarked, "Confederate commanders knew no more about the topography . . . within a day's march of the city of Richmond than they did about Central Africa."

Robert E. Lee once complained bitterly, "I cannot have my orders carried out."

For most of World War II the British armed forces fought with explosives much inferior, weight for weight, to those in German shells and bombs. Early in 1940, British scientists knew that the cheap, simple addition of a little powdered aluminum would double the power of existing explosives, yet the knowledge was not applied till late in 1943.

In the same war, the Australian commander of a hospital ship checked the vessel's water tanks after a refit and found them painted inside with red lead. It would have poisoned every man aboard.

These things—and hundreds more like them—I have seen and read about and heard about. I have accepted the universality of incompetence.

I have stopped being surprised when a moon rocket fails to get off the ground because something is forgotten, something breaks, something doesn't work, or something explodes prematurely.

I am no longer amazed to observe that a government-employed marriage counselor is a homosexual.

I now expect that statesmen will prove incompetent to fulfill their campaign pledges. I assume that if they do anything, it will probably be to carry out the pledges of their opponents.

This incompetence would be annoying enough if it were confined to public works, politics, space travel and such vast, remote fields of human endeavor. But it is not. It is close at hand, too—an ever-present, pestiferous nuisance.

As I write this page, the woman in the next apartment is talking on the telephone. I can hear every word she says. It is 10 P.M. and the man in the apartment on the other side of me has gone to bed early with a cold. I hear his intermittent cough. When he turns on his bed I hear the springs squeak. I don't live in a cheap rooming house: this is an expensive, modern, concrete high-rise apartment block. What's the matter with the people who designed and built it?

The other day a friend of mine bought a hacksaw, took it home and began to cut an iron bolt. At his second stroke, the saw blade snapped, and the adjustable joint of the frame broke so that it could not be used again.

Last week I wanted to use a tape recorder on the stage of a new high-school auditorium. I could get no power for the machine. The building engineer told me that, in a year's occupancy, he had been unable to find a switch that would turn on current in the base plugs on stage. He was beginning to think they were not wired up at all.

This morning I set out to buy a desk lamp. In a large furniture and appliance store I found a lamp that I liked. The salesman was going to wrap it, but I asked him to test it first. (I'm getting cautious nowadays.) He was obviously unused to testing electrical equipment, because it took him a long time to find a socket. Eventually he plugged the lamp in, then could not switch it on! He tried another lamp of the same style: that would not switch on, either. The whole consignment had defective switches. I left.

I recently ordered six hundred square feet of fiber glass insulation for a cottage I am renovating. I stood over the clerk at the order desk to make sure she got the quantity right. In vain! The building supply firm billed me for seven hundred square feet, and delivered nine hundred square feet!

Education, often touted as a cure for all ills, is apparently no cure for incompetence. Incompetence runs riot in the halls of education. One high-school graduate in three cannot read at normal fifth-grade level. It is now commonplace for colleges to be giving reading lessons to freshmen. In some colleges, *twenty percent* of freshmen cannot read well enough to understand their textbooks!

I receive mail from a large university. Fifteen months ago I changed my address. I sent the usual notice to the university: my mail kept going to the old address. After two more change-of-address notices and a phone call, I made a personal visit. I pointed with my finger to the wrong address in their records, dictated the new address and watched a secretary take it down. The mail still went to the old address. Two days ago there was a new development. I received a phone call from the woman who had succeeded me in my old apartment and who, of course, had been receiving my mail from the university. She herself has just moved again, and my mail from the university has now started going to *her* new address!

As I said, I became resigned to this omnipresent incompetence. Yet I thought that, if only its cause could be discovered, then a cure might be found. So I began asking questions.

I heard plenty of theories.

A banker blamed the schools: "Kids nowadays don't learn efficient work habits."

A teacher blamed politicians: "With such inefficiency at the seat of government, what can you expect from citizens? Besides, they resist our legitimate demands for adequate education budgets. If only we could get a computer in every school. . . ."

An atheist blamed the churches: ". . . drugging the people's minds with fables of a better world, and distracting them from practicalities."

A churchman blamed radio, television and movies: ". . . many distractions of modern life have drawn people away from the moral teachings of the church."

A trade unionist blamed management: ". . . too greedy to pay a living wage. A man can't take any interest in his job on this starvation pay."

A manager blamed unions: "The worker just doesn't care nowadays—thinks of nothing but raises, vacations and retirement pensions."

An individualist said that welfare-statism produces a general don't-care attitude. A social worker told me that moral laxity in the home and family breakdown produces irresponsibility on the job. A psychologist said that early repression of sexual impulses causes a subconscious desire to fail, as

Early repression of sexual impulses causes a subconscious desire to fail.

atonement for guilt feelings. A philosopher said, "Men are human; accidents will happen."

A multitude of different explanations is as bad as no explanation at all. I began to feel that I would never understand incompetence.

Then one evening, in a theatre lobby, during the second intermission of a dully performed play, I was grumbling about incompetent actors and directors, and got into conversation with Dr. Laurence J. Peter, a scientist who had devoted many years to the study of incompetence.

The intermission was too short for him to do more than whet my curiosity. After the show I went to his home and sat till 3:00 A.M. listening to his lucid, startlingly original exposition of a theory that at last answered my question, "Why incompetence?"

Dr. Peter exonerated Adam, agitators and accident, and arraigned one feature of our society as the perpetrator and rewarder of incompetence.

Incompetence explained! My mind flamed at the thought. Perhaps the next step might be incompetence eradicated!

With characteristic modesty, Dr. Peter had so far been satisfied to discuss his discovery with a few friends and colleagues and give an occasional lecture on his research. His vast collection of incompetenciana, his brilliant galaxy of incompetence theories and formulae, had never appeared in print.

"Possibly my Principle could benefit mankind," said Peter. "But I'm frantically busy with routine teaching and the associated paperwork; then there are faculty committee meetings, and my continuing research. Some day I may sort out the material and arrange it for publication, but for the next ten or fifteen years I simply won't have time."

I stressed the danger of procrastination and at last Dr. Peter agreed to a collaboration: he would place his extensive research reports and huge manuscript at my disposal; I would condense them into a book. The following pages present Professor Peter's explanation of his Principle, the most penetrating social and psychological discovery of the century.

Dare you read it?

Dare you face, in one blinding revelation, the reason why schools do not bestow wisdom, why governments cannot maintain order, why courts do not dispense justice, why prosperity fails to produce happiness, why utopian plans never generate utopias?

Do not decide lightly. The decision to read on is irrevocable. If you read, you can never regain your present state of blissful ignorance; you will never again unthinkingly venerate your superiors or dominate your subordinates. Never! The Peter Principle, once heard, cannot be forgotten.

What have you to gain by reading on? By conquering incompetence in yourself, and by understanding incompetence in others, you can do your own work more easily, gain promotion and make more money. You can avoid painful illnesses. You can become a leader of men. You can enjoy your leisure. You can gratify your friends, confound your enemies, impress your children and enrich and revitalize your marriage.

This knowledge, in short, will revolutionize your life—perhaps save it.

So, if you have courage, read on, mark, memorize and apply the Peter Principle.

CHAPTER I

The Peter Principle

"I begin to smell a rat."
M. DE CERVANTES

●

W<small>HEN</small> I was a boy I was taught that the men upstairs knew what they were doing. I was told, "Peter, the more you know, the further you go." So I stayed in school until I graduated from college and then went forth into the world clutching firmly these ideas and my new teaching certificate. During the first year of teaching I was upset to find that a number of teachers, school principals, supervisors and superintendents appeared to be unaware of their professional responsibilities and incompetent in executing their duties. For example my principal's main concerns were that all window shades be at the same level, that classrooms should be quiet and that no one step on or near the rose beds. The superintendent's main concerns were that no minority group, no matter how fanatical, should ever be offended and that all official forms be submitted on time. The children's education appeared farthest from the administrator mind.

At first I thought this was a special weakness of the school system in which I taught so I applied for certification

19

in another province. I filled out the special forms, enclosed the required documents and complied willingly with all the red tape. Several weeks later, back came my application and all the documents!

No, there was nothing wrong with my credentials; the forms were correctly filled out; an official departmental stamp showed that they had been received in good order. But an accompanying letter said, "The new regulations require that such forms cannot be accepted by the Department of Education unless they have been registered at the Post Office to ensure safe delivery. Will you please remail the forms to the Department, making sure to register them this time?"

I began to suspect that the local school system did not have a monopoly on incompetence.

As I looked further afield, I saw that every organization contained a number of persons who could not do their jobs.

A Universal Phenomenon

Occupational incompetence is everywhere. Have you noticed it? Probably we all have noticed it.

We see indecisive politicians posing as resolute statesmen and the "authoritative source" who blames his misinformation on "situational imponderables." Limitless are the public servants who are indolent and insolent; military commanders whose behavioral timidity belies their dreadnaught rhetoric, and governors whose innate servility prevents their actually governing. In our sophistication, we virtually shrug aside the immoral cleric, corrupt judge, incoherent attorney, author who cannot write and English teacher who cannot spell. At universities we see proclamations authored by administrators whose own office communications are

In our sophistication, we virtually shrug aside the immoral cleric.

hopelessly muddled; and droning lectures from inaudible or incomprehensible instructors.

Seeing incompetence at all levels of every hierarchy— political, legal, educational and industrial—I hypothesized that the cause was some inherent feature of the rules governing the placement of employees. Thus began my serious study of the ways in which employees move upward through a hierarchy, and of what happens to them after promotion.

For my scientific data hundreds of case histories were collected. Here are three typical examples.

MUNICIPAL GOVERNMENT FILE, CASE NO. 17   J. S. Minion * was a maintenance foreman in the public works department of Excelsior City. He was a favorite of the senior officials at City Hall. They all praised his unfailing affability.

"I like Minion," said the superintendent of works. "He has good judgment and is always pleasant and agreeable."

This behavior was appropriate for Minion's position: he was not supposed to make policy, so he had no need to disagree with his superiors.

The superintendent of works retired and Minion succeeded him. Minion continued to agree with everyone. He passed to his foreman every suggestion that came from above. The resulting conflicts in policy, and the continual changing of plans, soon demoralized the department. Complaints poured in from the Mayor and other officials, from taxpayers and from the maintenance-workers' union.

Minion still says "Yes" to everyone, and carries messages briskly back and forth between his superiors and his subordinates. Nominally a superintendent, he actually does the

---

* Some names have been changed, in order to protect the guilty.

work of a messenger. The maintenance department regularly exceeds its budget, yet fails to fulfill its program of work. In short, Minion, a competent foreman, became an incompetent superintendent.

SERVICE INDUSTRIES FILE, CASE NO. 3   E. Tinker was exceptionally zealous and intelligent as an apprentice at G. Reece Auto Repair Inc., and soon rose to journeyman mechanic. In this job he showed outstanding ability in diagnosing obscure faults, and endless patience in correcting them. He was promoted to foreman of the repair shop.

But here his love of things mechanical and his perfectionism become liabilities. He will undertake any job that he thinks looks interesting, no matter how busy the shop may be. "We'll work it in somehow," he says.

He will not let a job go until he is fully satisfied with it.

He meddles constantly. He is seldom to be found at his desk. He is usually up to his elbows in a dismantled motor and while the man who should be doing the work stands watching, other workmen sit around waiting to be assigned new tasks. As a result the shop is always overcrowded with work, always in a muddle, and delivery times are often missed.

Tinker cannot understand that the average customer cares little about perfection—he wants his car back on time! He cannot understand that most of his men are less interested in motors than in their pay checks. So Tinker cannot get on with his customers or with his subordinates. He was a competent mechanic, but is now an incompetent foreman.

MILITARY FILE, CASE NO. 8   Consider the case of the late renowned General A. Goodwin. His hearty, informal manner, his racy style of speech, his scorn for petty regulations and his undoubted personal bravery made him the idol of his men. He led them to many well-deserved victories.

When Goodwin was promoted to field marshal he had to deal, not with ordinary soldiers, but with politicians and allied generalissimos.

He would not conform to the necessary protocol. He could not turn his tongue to the conventional courtesies and flatteries. He quarreled with all the dignitaries and took to lying for days at a time, drunk and sulking, in his trailer. The conduct of the war slipped out of his hands into those of his subordinates. He had been promoted to a position that he was incompetent to fill.

An Important Clue!

In time I saw that all such cases had a common feature. The employee had been promoted from a position of competence to a position of incompetence. I saw that, sooner or later, this could happen to every employee in every hierarchy.

HYPOTHETICAL CASE FILE, CASE NO. 1   Suppose you own a pill-rolling factory, Perfect Pill Incorporated. Your foreman-pill roller dies of a perforated ulcer. You need a replacement. You naturally look among your rank-and-file pill rollers.

Miss Oval, Mrs. Cylinder, Mr. Ellipse and Mr. Cube all show various degrees of incompetence. They will naturally be ineligible for promotion. You will choose—other things being equal—your most competent pill roller, Mr. Sphere, and promote him to foreman.

Now suppose Mr. Sphere proves competent as foreman.

Later, when your general foreman, Legree, moves up to Works Manager, Sphere will be eligible to take his place.

If, on the other hand, Sphere is an incompetent foreman, he will get no more promotion. He has reached what I call his "level of incompetence." He will stay there till the end of his career.

Some employees, like Ellipse and Cube, reach a level of incompetence in the lowest grade and are never promoted. Some, like Sphere (assuming he is not a satisfactory foreman), reach it after one promotion.

E. Tinker, the automobile repair-shop foreman, reached his level of incompetence on the third stage of the hierarchy. General Goodwin reached his level of incompetence at the very top of the hierarchy.

So my analysis of hundreds of cases of occupational incompetence led me on to formulate *The Peter Principle:*

In a Hierarchy Every Employee Tends to Rise to His Level of Incompetence

A New Science!

Having formulated the Principle, I discovered that I had inadvertently founded a new science, hierarchiology, the study of hierarchies.

The term "hierarchy" was originally used to describe the system of church government by priests graded into ranks. The contemporary meaning includes any organization whose members or employees are arranged in order of rank, grade or class.

Hierarchiology, although a relatively recent discipline, appears to have great applicability to the fields of public and private administration.

This Means You!

My Principle is the key to an understanding of all hierarchal systems, and therefore to an understanding of the whole structure of civilization. A few eccentrics try to avoid getting involved with hierarchies, but everyone in business, industry, trade-unionism, politics, government, the armed forces, religion and education is so involved. All of them are controlled by the Peter Principle.

Many of them, to be sure, may win a promotion or two, moving from one level of competence to a higher level of competence. But competence in that new position qualifies them for still another promotion. For each individual, for

A few eccentrics try to avoid getting involved with hierarchies.

you, for *me,* the final promotion is from a level of competence to a level of incompetence.*

So, given enough time—and assuming the existence of enough ranks in the hierarchy—each employee rises to, and remains at, his level of incompetence. Peter's Corollary states:

In time, every post tends to be occupied by an employee who is incompetent to carry out its duties.

Who Turns the Wheels?

You will rarely find, of course, a system in which *every* employee has reached his level of incompetence. In most instances, something is being done to further the ostensible purposes for which the hierarchy exists.

Work is accomplished by those employees who have not yet reached their level of incompetence.

---

* The phenomena of "percussive sublimation" (commonly referred to as "being kicked upstairs") and of "the lateral arabesque" are not, as the casual observer might think, exceptions to the Principle. They are only pseudo-promotions, and will be dealt with in Chapter 3.

CHAPTER II

The Principle in Action

"To tell tales out of schoole"
J. HEYWOOD

A STUDY of a typical hierarchy, the Excelsior City school system, will show how the Peter Principle works within the teaching profession. Study this example and understand how hierarchiology operates within every establishment.

Let us begin with the rank-and-file classroom teachers. I group them, for this analysis, into three classes: competent, moderately competent and incompetent.

Distribution theory predicts, and experience confirms, that teachers will be distributed unevenly in these classes: the majority in the moderately competent class, minorities in the competent and incompetent classes. This graph illustrates the distribution:

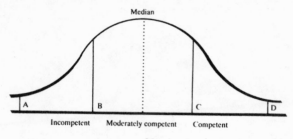

The Case of the Conformist

An incompetent teacher is ineligible for promotion. Dorothea D. Ditto, for example, had been an extremely conforming student in college. Her assignments were either plagiarisms from textbooks and journals, or transcriptions of the professors' lectures. She always did exactly as she was told, no more, no less. *She was considered to be a competent student.* She graduated with honors from the Excelsior Teachers' College.

When she became a teacher, she taught exactly as she herself had been taught. She followed precisely the textbook, the curriculum guide and the bell schedule.

Her work goes fairly well, except when no rule or precedent is available. For example, when a water pipe burst and flooded the classroom floor, Miss Ditto kept on teaching until the principal rushed in and rescued the class.

"Miss Ditto!" he cried. "In the Name of the Superintendent! There are three inches of water on this floor. Why is your class still here?"

She replied, "I didn't hear the emergency bell signal. I pay attention to those things. You know I do. I'm certain you didn't sound the bell." Flummoxed before the power of her awesome *non sequitur,* the principal invoked a provision of the school code giving him emergency powers in an extraordinary circumstance and led her sopping class from the building.

So, although she never breaks a rule or disobeys an order, she is often in trouble, and will never gain promotion. Competent as a student, *she has reached her level of incompetence as a classroom teacher, and will therefore remain in that position throughout her teaching career.*

The Eligible Majority

Most beginning teachers are moderately competent or competent—see the area from B to D on the graph—and *they will all be eligible for promotion.* Here is one such case.

A Latent Weakness

Mr. N. Beeker had been a competent student, and became a popular science teacher. His lessons and lab periods were inspiring. His students were co-operative and kept the laboratory in order. Mr. Beeker was not good at paper work, but this weakness was offset, in the judgment of his superiors, by his success as a teacher.

Beeker was promoted to head of the science department where he now had to order all science supplies and keep extensive records. *His incompetence is evident!* For three years running he has ordered new Bunsen burners, but no tubing for connecting them. As the old tubing deteriorates, fewer and fewer burners are operable, although new ones accumulate on the shelves.

Beeker is not being considered for further promotion. *His ultimate position is one for which he is incompetent.*

Higher up the Hierarchy

B. Lunt had been a competent student, teacher and department head, and was promoted to assistant principal. In this post he got on well with teachers, students and parents, and was intellectually competent. He gained a further promotion to the rank of principal.

Till now, he had never dealt directly with school-board members, or with the district superintendent of education. It soon appeared that he lacked the required finesse to work

He got on well with teachers, students and parents.

with these high officials. *He kept the superintendent waiting* while he settled a dispute between two children. Taking a class for a teacher who was ill, *he missed a curriculum revision committee meeting* called by the assistant superintendent.

He worked so hard at running his school that *he had no energy for running community organizations.* He declined offers to become program chairman of the Parent-Teacher Association, president of the Community Betterment League and consultant to the Committee for Decency in Literature.

His school lost community support and he fell out of favor with the superintendent. Lunt came to be regarded, by the public and by his superiors, as an incompetent principal. When the assistant superintendent's post became vacant, the school board declined to give it to Lunt. He remains, and will remain till he retires, unhappy and incompetent as a principal.

THE AUTOCRAT   R. Driver, having proved his competence as student, teacher, department head, assistant principal and principal, was promoted to assistant superintendent. Previously he had only to interpret the school board's policy and have it efficiently carried out in his school. Now, as assistant superintendent, he must participate in the policy discussions of the board, using democratic procedures.

But Driver dislikes democratic procedures. He insists on his status as an expert. He lectures the board members much as he used to lecture his students when he was a classroom teacher. He tries to dominate the board as he dominated his staff when he was a principal.

The board now considers Driver an incompetent assistant superintendent. He will receive no further promotion.

SOON PARTED   G. Spender was a competent student, English teacher, department head, assistant principal and principal. He then worked competently for six years as an assistant superintendent—patriotic, diplomatic, suave and well liked. He was promoted to superintendent. Here he was obliged to enter the field of school finance, in which he soon found himself at a loss.

From the start of his teaching career, Spender had never bothered his head about money. His wife handled his pay check, paid all household accounts and gave him pocket money each week.

Now Spender's incompetence in the area of finance is revealed. He purchased a large number of teaching machines from a fly-by-night company which went bankrupt without producing any programs to fit the machines. He had every classroom in the city equipped with television, although the only programs available in the area were for secondary schools. Spender has found his level of incompetence.

Another Promotion Mechanism

The foregoing examples are typical of what are called "line promotions." There is another mode of upward movement: the "staff promotion." The case of Miss T. Totland is typical.

Miss Totland, who had been a competent student and an outstanding primary teacher, was promoted to primary supervisor. She now has to teach, not children, but teachers. Yet *she still uses the techniques which worked so well with small children.*

Miss Totland had been an outstanding primary teacher.

Addressing teachers, singly or in groups, she speaks slowly and distinctly. She uses mostly words of one or two syllables. She explains each point several times in different ways, to be sure it is understood. She always wears a bright smile.

Teachers dislike what they call her false cheerfulness and her patronizing attitude. Their resentment is so sharp that, instead of trying to carry out her suggestions, they spend much time devising excuses for *not* doing what she recommends.

Miss Totland has proved herself incompetent in communicating with primary teachers. She is therefore ineligible for further promotion, *and will remain as primary supervisor, at her level of incompetence.*

You Be the Judge

You can find similar examples in any hierarchy. Look around you where you work, and pick out the people who have reached their level of incompetence. You will see that in every hierarchy *the cream rises until it sours.* Look in the mirror and ask whether . . .

No! You would prefer to ask, "Are there no exceptions to the Principle? Is there no escape from its operation?"

I shall discuss these questions in subsequent chapters.

CHAPTER III

Apparent Exceptions

*"When the case goes bad, the guilty man
Excepts, and thins his jury all he can."*

J. DRYDEN

———

M ANY people to whom I mention the Peter Principle do not want to accept it. They anxiously search for—and sometimes think they have found—flaws in my hierarchiological structure. So at this point I want to issue a warning: *do not be fooled by apparent exceptions.*

Apparent Exception No. 1: The Percussive Sublimation

"What about Walt Blockett's promotion? He was hopelessly incompetent, a bottleneck, so management *kicked him upstairs* to get him out of the road."

I often hear such questions. Let us examine this phenomenon, which I have named the *Percussive Sublimation.* Did Blockett move from a position of incompetence to a position of competence? No. He has simply been moved from

36

one unproductive position to another. Does he now undertake any greater responsibility than before? No. Does he accomplish any more work in the new position than he did in the old? No.

The percussive sublimation is a pseudo-promotion. Some Blockett-type employees actually believe that they have received a genuine promotion; others recognize the truth. But the main function of a pseudo-promotion is *to deceive people outside the hierarchy.* When this is achieved, the maneuver is counted a success.

But the experienced hierarchiologist will never be deceived. Hierarchiologically, the only move that we can accept as a genuine promotion is a move *from a level of competence.*

What is the effect of a successful percussive sublimation? Assume that Blockett's employer, Kickly, is still competent. Then by moving Blockett he achieves three goals:

1) He camouflages the ill-success of his promotion policy. To admit that Blockett was incompetent would lead observers to think, "Kickly should have realized, before giving Blockett that last promotion, that Blockett wasn't the man for the job." But a percussive sublimation *justifies the previous promotion* (in the eyes of employees and onlookers, not to a hierarchiologist).

2) He supports staff morale. Some employees at least, will think, "If *Blockett* can get a promotion, *I* can get a promotion." *One percussive sublimation serves as carrot-on-a-stick to many other employees.*

3) He maintains the hierarchy. Even though Blockett is incompetent, *he must not be fired:* he probably knows enough of Kickly's business to be dangerous in a competitive hierarchy.

A Common Phenomenon

Hierarchiology tells us that every thriving organization will be characterized by this accumulation of deadwood at the executive level, consisting of percussive sublimatees and potential candidates for percussive sublimation. One well-known appliance-manufacturing firm has twenty-three vice-presidents!

A Paradoxical Result!

The Waverley Broadcasting Corporation is noted for the creativity of its production department. This is made possible through percussive sublimation. Waverley has just moved all its non-creative, non-productive, redundant personnel into a palatial, three-million-dollar Head Office complex.

The Head Office contains no cameras, microphones or transmitters; indeed, it is miles away from the nearest studio. The people at Head Office are always frantically busy, drawing up reports and flow charts and making appointments to confer with one another.

Recently a reshuffle of senior officials was announced, aimed at streamlining the headquarters operation. Four vice-presidents were replaced by eight vice-presidents and a co-ordinating assistant to the president.

So we see that the percussive sublimation can serve *to keep the drones out of the hair of the workers!*

Apparent Exception No. 2: The Lateral Arabesque

The lateral arabesque is another pseudo-promotion. Without being raised in rank—sometimes without even a pay raise—the incompetent employee is given *a new and longer title* and is moved to an office in a remote part of the building.

R. Filewood proved incompetent as office manager of Cardley Stationery Inc. After a lateral arabesque he found himself, at the same salary, working as co-ordinator of inter-departmental communications, supervising the filing of second copies of inter-office memos.

AUTOMOTIVE MANUFACTURING FILE, CASE NO. 8 Wheeler Automobile Parts Ltd. has developed the lateral arabesque more fully than most hierarchies. The Wheeler operations are divided into many regions, and at last count, I found that twenty-five senior executives had been banished to the provinces as regional vice-presidents.

The company bought a motel and ordered one senior official to go and run it.

Another redundant vice-president has been laboring for three years to write the company's history.

I conclude that *the larger the hierarchy, the easier is the lateral arabesque.*

A CASE OF LEVITATION The entire 82-man staff of a small government department was moved away to another department, leaving the director, at $16,000 a year, with *nothing to do* and *nobody to supervise.* Here we see the rare phenomenon of a hierarchal pyramid consisting solely of the capstone, suspended aloft without a base to support it! This interesting condition I denominate the *free-floating apex.*

Apparent Exception No. 3: Peter's Inversion

A friend of mine was travelling in a country where the sale of alcoholic beverages is a government monopoly. Just before returning home he went to a government liquor store and asked, "How much liquor am I allowed to take back home with me?"

"You'll have to ask the Customs officers at the border," said the clerk.

"But I want to know *now*," said the traveller, "so that I can buy all the liquor that is permissible, and yet not buy too much and get some of it confiscated."

"It's a Customs regulation," replied the clerk. "It's nothing to do with us."

"But surely *you know* the Customs regulation," said the traveller.

"Yes, I know it," said the clerk, "but Customs regulations are not a responsibility of this department so I'm not allowed to tell you."

Have you ever had a similar experience, ever been told, "We don't give out that information"? The official knows the answer to your problem; you know that he knows it; but for some reason or other, he won't tell you.

Once, taking a professorship at a new university, I received a special identification card, issued by the payroll department of the university, entitling me to cash checks at the university book store. I went to the store, presented my card, and proffered a twenty-dollar American Express traveller's check.

"We only cash payroll checks and personal checks," said the book-store cashier.

"But this is better than a personal check," I said. "It's better even than a payroll check. I can cash this in any store even without this special card. A traveller's check is as good as cash."

"But it's not a payroll check or a personal check," said the cashier.

After a little more discussion, I asked to see the manager. He listened to me patiently, but with a faraway expression, then stated flatly. "We do not cash traveller's checks."

You have heard of hospitals which spend precious time filling in sheaves of forms before helping accident victims. You have heard of the nurse who says, "Wake up! It's time to take your sleeping pill."

You may have read of the Irishman, Michael Patrick O'Brien, who was kept for eleven months on a ferryboat plying between Hong Kong and Macao. He did not have the correct papers to get off at either end of the trip, and nobody would issue them to him.

Particularly among minor officials with no discretionary powers, one sees an obsessive concern with getting forms filled out correctly, whether the forms serve any useful purpose or not. No deviation, however slight, from the customary routine, will be permitted.

Professional Automatism

The above type of behavior I call *professional automatism*. To the professional automaton it is clear that means are more important than ends; the paperwork is more important than the purpose for which it was originally designed. He no longer sees himself as existing to serve the public: he sees the public as the raw material that serves to maintain him, the forms, the rituals and the hierarchy!

The professional automaton, from the viewpoint of his customers, clients or victims, seems incompetent. So you will no doubt be wondering, *"How do so many professional automatons win promotion? And is the professional automaton outside the operation of the Peter Principle?"*

To answer those questions I must first pose another: "Who defines competence?"

A Question of Standards

The competence of an employee is determined *not by outsiders but by his superior in the hierarchy.* If the superior is still at a level of competence, he may evaluate his subordinates in terms of the performance of useful work—for example, the supplying of medical services or information, the production of sausages or table legs or achieving whatever are the stated aims of the hierarchy. That is to say, *he evaluates output.*

But if the superior has reached his level of incompetence, he will probably rate his subordinates in terms of institutional values: he will see competence as the behavior that supports the rules, rituals and forms of the status quo. Promptness, neatness, courtesy to superiors, internal paperwork, will be highly regarded. In short, such an official *evaluates input.*

"Rockman is *dependable.*"

"Lubrik contributes to the *smooth running* of the office."

"Rutter is *methodical.*"

"Miss Trudgen is a *steady, consistent* worker."

"Mrs. Friendly *co-operates* well with colleagues."

In such instances, *internal consistency is valued more highly than efficient service:* this is *Peter's Inversion.* A professional automaton may also be termed a "Peter's Invert." He has inverted the means-end relationship.

Now you can understand the actions of the Peter's Inverts described earlier.

If the liquor-store clerk had promptly explained the Customs regulations, the traveller would have thought, "How courteous!" But his superior would have marked the clerk down for breaking a rule of the department.

If the book-store cashier had accepted my traveller's check, I would have considered him helpful: the manager would have reprimanded him for exceeding his authority.

Promotion Prospects for Peter's Inverts

The Peter's Invert or professional automaton has, as we have seen, little capacity for independent judgment. He *always obeys, never decides*. This, from the viewpoint of the hierarchy, is competence, so the Peter's Invert is eligible for promotion. He will continue to rise unless some mischance places him in a post where he has to make decisions. Here he will find his level of incompetence.*

We see therefore that professional automatism—however annoying you may have found it—is not, after all, an exception to the Peter Principle. As I often tell my students, "Competence, like truth, beauty and contact lenses, is in the eye of the beholder."

---

* There are two kinds of minor decisions which I have sometimes seen made by promoted Peter's Inverts:

a) to tighten up on enforcement of regulations
b) to make new regulations covering a marginal case which does not exactly fit existing regulations.

These actions only serve to strengthen the inversion.

Apparent Exception No. 4: Hierarchal Exfoliation

Next I shall discuss a case which to untrained observers is perhaps the most puzzling of all: the case of the brilliant, productive worker who not only wins no promotion, but is even dismissed from his post.

Let me give a few examples; then I will explain them.

In Excelsior City every new schoolteacher is placed on one year's probation. K. Buchman had been a brilliant English scholar at the university. In his probationary year of English teaching, he managed to infuse his students with his own enthusiasm for classical and modern literature. Some of them obtained Excelsior City Public Library cards; some began to haunt new- and used-book stores. They became so interested that they read many books that were not on the Excelsior Schools Approved Reading List.

Before long, several irate parents and delegations from two austere religious sects visited the school superintendent to complain that their children were studying "undesirable" literature. Buchman was told that his services would not be required the following year.

Probationer-teacher C. Cleary's first teaching assignment was to a special class of retarded children. Although he had been warned that these children would not accomplish very much, he proceeded to teach them all he could. By the end of the year, many of Cleary's retarded children scored better on standardized achievement tests of reading and arithmetic than did children in regular classes.

When Cleary received his dismissal notice he was told that he had grossly neglected the bead stringing, sandbox and other busy-work which were the things that retarded children should do. He had failed to make adequate use of the modelling clay, pegboards and finger paints specially provided by the Excelsior City Special Education Department.

Miss E. Beaver, a probationer primary teacher, was highly gifted intellectually. Being inexperienced, she put into practice what she had learned at college about making allowances for pupils' individual differences. As a result, her brighter pupils finished two or three years' work in one year.

The principal was very courteous when he explained that Miss Beaver could not be recommended for permanent engagement. He knew she would understand that she had upset the system, had not stuck to the course of studies, and had created hardship for the children who would not fit into the next year's program. She had disrupted the official marking system and textbook-issuing system, and had caused severe anxiety to the teacher who would next year have to handle the children who had already covered the work.

The Paradox Explained

These cases illustrate the fact that, in most hierarchies, *super-competence is more objectionable than incompetence.*

Ordinary incompetence, as we have seen, is no cause for dismissal: it is simply a bar to promotion. Super-competence often leads to dismissal, *because it disrupts the hierarchy,* and thereby violates *the first commandment* of hierarchal life: *the hierarchy must be preserved.*

You will recall that in Chapter 2 I discussed three classes of employees: the incompetent, the moderately competent and the competent. At that time, for simplicity's sake, I chopped off the two extremes of the distribution curve and omitted two more classes of employees. Here is the complete curve.

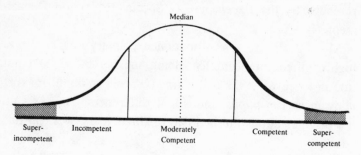

Employees in the two extreme classes—the super-competent and the super-incompetent—are alike subject to dismissal. They are usually fired soon after being hired, for the same reason: that they tend to disrupt the hierarchy. This sloughing off of extremes is called *Hierarchal Exfoliation*.

Some Horrible Examples

I have already described the fate of some super-competent employees. Here are some examples of super-incompetence.

Miss P. Saucier was hired as a salesgirl in the appliance department of the Lomark Department Store. From the start she sold less than the average amount of merchandise. This alone would not have been cause for dismissal, because many other salespeople were below average. But Miss Saucier's record keeping was atrocious: she punched wrong keys on the cash register, accepted competitors' credit cards and—still worse—inserted the carbon paper with the wrong side up when filling in a sales-contract form. She then managed to give the customer the original of the contract. He

W. Kirk held radical views on the nature of the Deity.

left with the two records (one on the front of the contract and the other in reverse on the back) and she was left with none. Worst of all, she was insolent to her superiors. She was dismissed after one month.

W. Kirk, a Protestant clergyman, held radical views on the nature of the Deity, the efficacy of the sacraments, the second coming of Christ, and life after death—views sharply opposed to the official doctrines of his sect. Technically, then, Kirk was incompetent to give his parishioners the spiritual guidance they expected. He received no promotion, of course; nevertheless he retained his post for several years. Then he wrote a book which condemned the stodgy church hierarchy and propounded a reasoned argument favoring taxation of all churches. He asked that ecclesiastical recognition be extended to such social problems as homosexuality, drug abuses, racial injustices and the like. . . . He had moved, at one jump, from incompetence to super-incompetence, and was promptly dismissed.

The super-incompetent exfoliate must have two important characteristics:

1) he fails to produce (output).
2) he fails to support internal consistency of the hierarchy (input).

Is Exfoliation for You?

We see, then, that super-competence and super-incompetence are equally objectionable to the typical hierarchy.

We see, too, that hierarchal exfoliates, like all other employees, are subject to the Peter Principle.

They differ from other employees in being the only types who, under present conditions, are subject to dismissal.

Would you like to be somewhere else? Is your present placement in military service, school or business your choice or are you a victim of legal or family pressure? With planning and determination *you, too,* can make yourself either super-competent or super-incompetent.

Apparent Exception No. 5: The Paternal In-Step

Some owners of old-fashioned family businesses used to treat their sons like regular employees. The boy would start at the bottom of the hierarchy and rise in accordance with the Peter Principle. Here, of course, the owner's love for his hierarchy, his desire to keep it efficient and profitable, and his stern sense of justice, outweighed his natural familial affections.

Often, though, the owner of such a business would bring his son in at a high level with the idea that in time, without rising through the ranks, he should take over the supreme command or, as the phrase went, should "step into his father's shoes."

This type of placement, therefore, I call *The Paternal In-Step.*

There are two principal means by which the Paternal In-Step is executed.

P.I-S Method No. 1

An existing employee may be dismissed or removed by lateral arabesque or percussive sublimation, to make a place for the In-Stepper. Used less often than Method No. 2, this technique may cause considerable ill-feeling toward the new appointee.

P.I-S Method No. 2

A new position, with an impressive title, is created for the In-Stepper.

The Method Explained

The Paternal In-Step is merely a small-scale example of the situation that exists under a class system, where certain favored individuals enter a hierarchy above the class barrier, instead of at the bottom.*

The infusion of new employees at a high level may some-times increase output. The Paternal In-Step, therefore, arouses no ill-feeling outside the hierarchy.

Yet the arrival of the In-Stepper is to a degree resented by other members of the hierarchy. Employees actually have a sentimental feeling (Peter's Penchant) for the promotion process by which they themselves have risen and by which they hope to rise further. They tend to resent placements made by other means.

The Paternal In-Step Today

The family business, controlled by one man with the authority to place his sons in its higher ranks, is nowadays something of a rarity. Nevertheless, the Paternal In-Step is still executed in just the same way, except that the In-Stepper need not be related to the official who appoints him.

Let me cite a typical example.

PATERNAL IN-STEP FILE, CASE NO. 7   A. Purefoy, Director of the Excelsior City Health and Sanitation Department,

---

* For full discussion of the operation of hierarchies under a class-system, see Chapter 7.

found that by the end of one financial year he was going to have some unexpended funds. The citizens had suffered no epidemics; the Excelsior River had not, as it often did, overflowed its banks and silted up the drainage system; both his assistant directors (one for health, the other for sanitation) were earnest, competent, economically minded men.

So the budgeted funds had not been spent. Purefoy realized that unless he took rapid action he would suffer a cut in the coming year's budget.

He determined to create a third assistant directorship whose incumbent would organize an Anti-Litter and City Beautification Program. To fill the new post he engaged W. Pickwick, a young graduate from the School of Business Administration of his own alma mater.

Pickwick, in turn, created eleven more new posts: an anti-litter supervisor, six litter inspectors, a three-girl office staff, and a public relations officer.

N. Wordsworth, the P.R.O., organized essay contests for school children, adult contests for jingles and poster designs, and commissioned two films, one of anti-litter propaganda, the other on city beautification. The films were to be made by an independent producer who had been with Wordsworth and Pickwick in the university dramatic society.

Everything worked out well: Director Purefoy exceeded his budget and was successful in obtaining a larger budget for the following year.

Modern Father Substitutes

Nowadays governments set up the "Father's Shoe Situation." Federal grants are offered for many new purposes—war on pollution, war on poverty, war on illiteracy, war on loneliness, war on illegitimacy and research into the recreational potential of interplanetary space travel for the culturally disadvantaged.

As soon as money is offered, a way must be found to spend it. A new position is created—anti-poverty co-ordinator, head-start director, book-selection advisor, organizer for Senior Citizens' Welfare and Happiness Projects, or what have you. Someone is recruited to occupy the position, to wear, if not necessarily to *fill,* the shoes.

The In-Stepper may or may not solve the problem that he was set to solve: that does not matter. The important point is that he must be able and willing to spend the money.

The Principle Not Breached

Such a placement is in accordance with the Peter Principle. Competence or incompetence is irrelevant so long as the shoes are filled. If they are filled competently the In-Stepper will in time be eligible to step up and out of them and find his level of incompetence on a higher plane.

Conclusions

The apparent exceptions *are not exceptions.* The Peter Principle applies to all employees in all hierarchies.

CHAPTER IV

Pull & Promotion

"A long pull, and a strong pull, and a pull all together."

C. DICKENS

Y ou have seen that the Peter Principle is immutable and universal but you may still want to know how long your hierarchal ascension will take. Chapters 4 and 5 will help reveal this to you. First let us turn our attention to accelerated elevation through pull.

"Pull" Defined in Sixteen Words

I define Pull as "an employee's relationship—by blood, marriage or acquaintance—with a person above him in the hierarchy."

Unpopularity of the Pullee

Winning promotion through Pull is a thing we all hate— *in other people*. Co-workers dislike the beneficiary of Pull (the Pullee) and usually express that dislike in comments on his incompetence.

Soon after W. Kinsman became superintendent of schools in Excelsior City, his son-in-law, L. Harker, was promoted to the post of music supervisor. Some teachers criticized this appointment on the ground that Harker was *hard of hearing!* They said the music supervisor's post belonged by right of seniority (input) to D. Roane.

ENVY KNOWS NO LOGIC   D. Roane had listened so long to so many school choirs and orchestras that *he hated music and children!* Obviously, he would have been no more competent (in terms of output) than Harker as music supervisor.

The teacher's resentment, then, was not really against Harker's incompetence, but against his violation of the time-honored seniority system.

Employees in a hierarchy do not really object to incompetence (Peter's Paradox): they merely gossip about incompetence to mask their envy of employees who have Pull.

How to Acquire Pull

One may study the careers of many employees who had Pull (Pullees), comparing them with employees of equal ability who had none. The results of my research can be reduced to five practical suggestions for the would-be Pullee.

1. Find a Patron

A Patron is a person above you in the hierarchy who can help you to rise. Sometimes you may have to do a good deal of scouting to find who has, and who has not, this power. You may think that your promotion rate depends on the good or bad reports written about you by your immediate superior. This *may be* correct. But management *may be* aware that your immediate superior is already at his level of incompetence, and therefore may attach *little importance*

A patron is a person above you in the hierarchy who can help you to rise.

to his recommendations, favorable or otherwise! So do not be superficial: dig deep, and ye shall find.

2. Motivate the Patron

"An unmotivated Patron is no Patron." See that the Patron has *something to gain* by assisting you, or *something to lose* by not assisting you, to rise in the hierarchy.

My research has yielded many examples of this motivation process, some charming, some sordid. I shall not cite them. I would rather make this point a test for the reader, a test which I call *Peter's Bridge*. If you cannot cross it under your own steam, you have already reached your level of incompetence and no advice from me can help you.

3. Get Out from Under

"There's no road like the open road."

Imagine you are at a swimming pool, trying to climb to the high diving board. Halfway up the ladder, your ascent is blocked by a would-be diver who began to climb but has now lost his nerve. Eyes shut, he clings desperately to the handrail. He will not fall off, but he cannot go higher, and you cannot pass him. Encouraging shouts from your friend already on the top board are of no avail in this situation.

Similarly, in an occupational hierarchy, neither your own efforts, nor the Pull of your Patron, can help you if the next step above you is blocked by someone at his level of incompetence (a Super-incumbent). This awkward situation I denominate *Peter's Pretty Pass*. (Things have come to a pretty pass, etc.)

Let us return mentally to the swimming pool. To reach the top of the diving board, you would get off the ladder that is blocked, cross over to the ladder on the other side, and climb without hindrance to the top.

To move up the job hierarchy, you get out from under the Super-incumbent and move into a promotion channel that is not blocked. This maneuver is called *Peter's Circumambulation.*

Before investing time and effort in Peter's Circumambulation, make sure that you really are in Peter's Pretty Pass—*i.e.*, that the man above you is a genuine Super-incumbent. If he is still eligible for promotion, he is not a Super-incumbent: you need not dodge round him. Simply exert a little patience, wait a while; he will be promoted, a gap will open up and Pull will be able to do its wondrous work.

To discover, without any doubt, whether your superior is a Super-incumbent, look for the medical and non-medical indices of Final Placement, which are described in Chapters 11 and 12 of this book.

4. Be Flexible

There is only so much that any one Patron can do for you. To draw an analogy, an experienced mountaineer can pull a weaker climber up to his level. Then the leader must himself climb higher before he can exert more pull.

But if the first Patron *cannot climb higher,* then the Pullee must find another Patron who can.

So be prepared, when the time comes, to switch your allegiance to another Patron of higher rank than the first.

"There's no Patron like a new Patron!"

5. Obtain Multiple Patronage

"The combined Pull of several Patrons is the sum of their separate Pulls multiplied by the number of Patrons." (Hull's Theorem.) The multiplication effect occurs because the Patrons talk among themselves and constantly reinforce in one another their opinions of your merits, and their determination to do something for you. With a single Patron, you get none of this reinforcement effect. "Many a Patron makes a promotion."

Why Wait? Escalate!!!

By following these hints, *you can obtain Pull*. Pull will speed your upward motion through the hierarchy. It can bring you to your level much sooner.

CHAPTER V

Push & Promotion

*"Slump, and the world slumps with you.
Push and you push alone."*

N EXT let us see how far an employee's promotion rate
can be affected by the force of Push.

There has been much misunderstanding about the function of Push, largely because of the persistence of Alger * in
exaggerating the efficiency of Push as a means to promotion.
One must indeed deplore the unscientific, misguided zeal of
Alger's work, and its retarding effect on the science of hierarchiology.

Peale,† too, seems to overestimate the effect of Push.

A Fallacy Exploded

My surveys show that, in established organizations, the
downward pressure of the Seniority Factor nullifies the upward force of Push. This observation, by the way, shows that
Pull is stronger than Push. Pull often overcomes the Seniority
Factor. Push seldom does so.

---

* Alger, Horatio, Jr. (1832–99). *Struggling Upward, Slow and Sure,*
and many other works.

† Peale, Norman V. (1898–19——). *The Power of Positive Thinking,*
New York: Prentice-Hall, 1952, and many other works.

Push alone cannot extricate you from Peter's Pretty Pass. Push alone will not enable you to successfully execute Peter's Circumambulation. Using the Circumambulation without the aid of Pull simply makes superiors say, "He can't apply himself to anything for very long." "No stick-to-itiveness!" etc.

Neither can Push have any effect on ultimate placement level. That is because all employees, aggressive or shy, are subject to the Peter Principle, and must sooner or later come to rest at their level of incompetence.

Signs and Symptoms of Push

Push is sometimes manifested by an abnormal interest in study, vocational training and self-improvement courses. (In marginal cases, and particularly in small hierarchies, such training may increase competence to a point where promotion is slightly accelerated. The effect is imperceptible in large hierarchies, where the Seniority Factor is stronger.)

Perils of Push

Study and self-improvement may even have a negative effect if increased areas of competence result in the employee's requiring a larger number of promotional steps to reach his level of incompetence.

Suppose, for example, that B. Sellers, a competent local sales representative for Excelsior Mattress Co., managed, by hard study, to master a foreign language. It is quite possible that he would then have to fill one or more posts in the company's overseas sales organization before being brought home and promoted to his final position of incompetence as sales manager. Study created a detour in Sellers' hierarchal flight plan.

The Final Verdict

In my judgment, the positive and negative effects of study and training tend to cancel each other. The same applies to other manifestations of Push such as starting work early and staying late. The admiration inspired in some colleagues by these semi-Machiavellian ploys will ultimately be balanced by the detestation it elicits from others.

An Exception That Proves the Rule

You do occasionally find an exceptionally pushful employee who manages, by fair means or foul, to oust a Superincumbent, and so clear a place for himself on a higher rank, sooner than natural processes would have done it.

W. Shakespeare cites an interesting example in *Othello*. In Act I, Scene 1, the ambitious Iago bemoans the fact that promotion is determined by pull, not by strict rules of seniority:

> *. . . 'tis the curse of service,*
> *Preferment goes by letter and affection,*
> *And not by old gradation, where each second*
> *Stood heir to the first.*

The promotion that Iago wants is given instead to Michael Cassio. So Iago contrives a double plan, to murder Cassio and to discredit him in the eyes of the commanding officer, Othello.

The plan comes near to success, but Iago's wife, Emilia, is an incorrigible blabbermouth:

> *Let heaven and men and devils, let them all,*
> *All, all cry shame against me, yet I'll speak.*

She gives the game away, and Iago never receives the coveted promotion.

We should learn by Iago's fate that *secrecy is the soul of Push*.

Pushfulness of this degree, however, is quite rare; it cannot seriously alter my assessment of the Push Factor.

A Dangerous Delusion

There are two reasons why the power of Push is so often overestimated. First is the obsessive feeling that a person who pushes harder than average deserves to advance farther and faster than average.

This feeling, of course, has no scientific basis: it is simply a moralistic delusion that I call *The Alger Complex.**

The Medical Aspect

Second, to unskilled observers, the power of Push sometimes seems greater than it really is because *many pushful persons exhibit the Pseudo-Achievement Syndrome.*

They suffer from such complaints as nervous breakdowns, peptic ulcers and insomnia. An ulcer, the badge of administrative success, may only be the product of pushfulness.

Colleagues who do not understand the situation may classify such a patient as an example of the Final Placement Syndrome (see Chapter 11) and may think that he has achieved final placement.

In fact, these people often have several ranks and several years of promotion potential ahead of them.

An Important Distinction

The difference between cases of Pseudo-Achievement Syndrome and Final Placement Syndrome is known as

---

* *Ibid.*

Peter's Nuance. For your own guidance in classifying such cases, you should always ask yourself, "Is the person accomplishing any useful work?" If the answer is:

a) "YES"—he has not reached his level of incompetence and therefore exhibits only the Pseudo-Achievement Syndrome.

b) "NO" he *has* reached his level of incompetence, and therefore exhibits the Final Placement Syndrome.

c) "DON'T KNOW"—*you* have reached *your* level of incompetence. Examine yourself for symptoms at once!

Last Words on Push

Never stand when you can sit; never walk when you can ride; never Push when you can Pull.

CHAPTER VI

Followers
& Leaders

"Consider what precedes and what follows."

P. SYRUS

─────────────────

Bang! Bang!

One urgent task I have had to face is the exploding of
various fallacies that still linger on from the pre-scientific
era of hierarchiology.

What could be more misleading, for example, than "Nothing succeeds like success"?

As you already understand, hierarchiology clearly shows
that *nothing fails like success,* when an employee rises to his
level of incompetence.

Later, when I discuss Creative Incompetence, I shall show
that *nothing succeeds like failure.*

But in this chapter I shall particularly discuss the old saw,
"You have to be a good follower to be a good leader."

This is typical of the hierarchiological fallacies bandied
about in administrative circles. For instance, when asked to
comment on how her son achieved his military prowess,
George Washington's mother answered, "I taught him to

64

obey." America was thus presented with one more *non sequitur*. How can the ability to lead depend on the ability to follow? You might as well say that the ability to float depends on the ability to sink.

From Underdog to Upperdog

Take the simplest possible case: a hierarchy with two ranks. The employee who proves himself good at obeying orders will get promotion to the rank where his job is to give orders.

The same principle holds true in more complex hierarchies: competent followers show high promotion potential in the lower ranks, but eventually reveal their incompetence as leaders.

A recent survey of business failures showed that 53 percent were due to plain managerial incompetence! These were the former followers, trying to be leaders.

MILITARY FILE, CASE NO. 17   Captain N. Chatters competently filled an administrative post at an army base. He worked well with all ranks and obeyed orders cheerfully and exactly. In short, he was a good follower. He was promoted to the rank of major, and now had to work largely on his own initiative.

But Chatters could not endure the measure of solitude that necessarily accompanies a position of authority. He would hang around his subordinates, gossiping and joking with them, interfering with the performance of their work. He was quite unable to give someone an order and *let him get on with it:* he had to butt in with unwanted advice. Under this harassment, Chatters' subordinates became inefficient and unhappy.

Chatters also spent much time loitering around the office of his colonel. When he could find no legitimate reason for talking to the C.O., he would gossip with the C.O.'s secretary. She could not very well tell him to clear out and leave her alone. Her work slipped into arrears.

To get rid of Chatters the colonel would set him running errands all over the base.

In this instance, a good follower promoted to a position of leadership:

a) Fails to exercise leadership

b) Reduces efficiency among his subordinates

c) Wastes the time of his superiors

SELF-MADE MEN FILE, CASE NO. 2   In most hierarchies, as a matter of fact, employees with the greatest leadership potential cannot become leaders. Let me cite an example.

W. Wheeler was a bicycle delivery boy in the Mercury Messenger Service. Wheeler systematized his delivery work to an unprecedented degree. For example, he explored and mapped every passable lane, alley and short-cut in his territory; he timed with a stop watch the periods of all the traffic lights, so that he could plan his route to avoid delays.

As a result, he always delivered his daily quota of packages with two hours or more to spare, and spent the time sitting in cafés reading books on business management. When he began reorganizing the routes of the other messenger boys, he was fired.

For the moment, he seemed to be a failure, an example of the super-incompetent hierarchal exfoliate, a living testimony to the "poor-follower-poor-leader" theory.

But soon he formed a concern of his own, Pegasus Flying

Wheeler systematized his delivery work to an unprecedented degree.

Deliveries, and within three years drove Mercury out of business.

So we see that exceptional leadership competence cannot make its way within an established hierarchy. It usually breaks out of the hierarchy and starts afresh somewhere else.

FAMOUS NAMES FILE, CASE NO. 902   T. A. Edison, fired for incompetence as a newsboy, founded, and successfully led, his own organization.

A Rare Exception

Occasionally, in special circumstances, leadership potential may be recognized. For example, in an army at war, all the officers of a certain unit were killed in a night attack. L. Dare, a corporal, assumed command, repulsed the enemy and led his comrades to safety. He was promoted in the field.

Dare would not have gained such a promotion in peace-time: he showed too much initiative. He was promoted only because the normal system of ranks and seniority had been disrupted and the hierarchy destroyed or temporarily suspended.

But How about the Principle?

At this point you may be feeling baffled, wondering whether I am not undermining the Peter Principle, which of course states that a competent employee is always eligible for promotion. There is no contradiction!

As we saw in Chapter 3, an employee's competence is assessed, not by disinterested observers like you and me, but by the employer or—more likely nowadays—by other employees on higher ranks of the same hierarchy. In their eyes, leadership potential is insubordination, and insubordination is incompetence.

Good followers do not become good leaders. To be sure, the good follower may win many promotions, but that does not make him a leader. Most hierarchies are nowadays so cumbered with rules and traditions, and so bound in by public laws, that even high employees do not have to lead anyone anywhere, in the sense of pointing out the direction and setting the pace. They simply follow precedents, obey regulations, and move at the head of the crowd. Such employees *lead* only in the sense that the *carved wooden figurehead leads the ship.*

It is easy to see how, in such a milieu, the advent of a genuine leader will be feared and resented. This is called *Hypercaninophobia* (top-dog fear) or more correctly by advanced hierarchiologists the *Hypercaninophobia Complex* (fear that the underdog may become the top dog).

CHAPTER VII

Hierarchiology & Politics

*"The history of mankind is an immense sea of errors
in which a few obscure truths may here and there be found."*

C. DE BECCARIA

W<small>E</small> have seen how the Peter Principle operates in some simple hierarchies—school systems, factories, auto-repair shops and so on. Now let us examine the more complex hierarchies of politics and government.

During one of my lectures a Latin-American student, Caesare Innocente, said, "Professor Peter, I'm afraid that what I want to know is not answered by all my studying. I don't know whether the world is run by smart men who are, how you Americans say, putting us on, or by imbeciles who really mean it." Innocente's question summarizes the thoughts and feelings that many have expressed. Social sciences have failed to provide consistent answers.

No political theorist so far has satisfactorily analyzed the workings of governments, or has accurately predicted the political future. The Marxists have proved as wrong in their analysis as have the capitalist theoreticians. My studies in comparative hierarchiology have shown that capitalistic, socialistic, and communistic systems are characterized by the same accumulation of redundant and incompetent personnel. Although my research is incomplete at this time, I submit the following as an interim report. If funds are made available, I will complete my research on comparative hierarchiology. When this is done I intend to study *universal hierarchiology.*

Interim Report·

In any economic or political crisis, one thing is certain. *Many learned experts* will prescribe *many different remedies.*

The budget won't balance: A. says, "Raise taxes," B. cries, "Reduce taxes."

Foreign investors are losing confidence in the dollar: C. urges tight money, while D. advocates inflation.

There are riots in the streets. E. proposes to subsidize the poor; F. calls for encouragement of the rich.

A foreign power makes threatening noises. G. says, "Defy him." H. says, "Conciliate him."

Why the Confusion?

1) Many of the experts have actually reached their level of incompetence: their advice is nonsensical or irrelevant.

2) Some of them have sound theories, but are unable to put them into effect.

3) In any event, neither sound nor unsound proposals can be carried out efficiently, because the machinery of gov-

ernment is a vast series of interlocking hierarchies, riddled through and through with incompetence.

Let us consider two of the branches of government—the legislature which frames laws, and the executive which, through its army of civil servants, tries to enforce them.

The Legislature

Most modern legislatures—even in the undemocratic countries—are elected by popular vote. One might think that the voters would, in their own interests, recognize and elect the most competent statesmen to represent them at the capital. That is, indeed, the simplified theory of representative government. In reality, the process is somewhat more complicated.

Present-day politics is dominated by the party system. Some countries have only one official party; some have two; some have several. A political party is usually naïvely pictured as a group of like-minded people co-operating to further their common interests. This is no longer valid. That function is now carried on entirely by *the lobby,* and there are as many lobbies as there are special interests.

A political party now exists primarily as *an apparatus for selecting candidates* and getting them elected to office.

A Dying Breed

To be sure, one occasionally sees an "independent" candidate get elected by his own efforts, without party endorsement. But the enormous expense of political campaigning makes this phenomenon rare enough at the local and regional levels, and unknown in national elections. It is fair to say that parties dominate the selection of candidates in modern politics.

The Party Hierarchy

Each political party, as any member knows, is a hierarchy. Admittedly, most members work for nothing, even pay for the privilege, but there is nevertheless a well-marked structure of ranks and a definite system of promotion from rank to rank.

I have so far shown the Peter Principle in its application to paid workers. You will see now that it is valid in this type of hierarchy, too.

In a political party, as in a factory or an army, competence in one rank is a requisite for promotion to the next. A competent door-to-door canvasser becomes eligible for promotion; he may be allowed to organize a team of canvassers. The ineffective or obnoxious canvasser continues knocking on doors, alienating voters.

A fast envelope stuffer may expect to become captain of an envelope-stuffing team; an incompetent envelope stuffer will remain, slowly and awkwardly stuffing envelopes, putting two leaflets in some, none in others, folding the leaflets wrongly, dropping them on the floor, and so on, as long as he stays with the party.

A competent fund raiser may be promoted to the committee which nominates the candidate. Although he was a good beggar, he may not be a competent judge of men as lawmakers and may support an incompetent candidate.

Even if a majority of the nominating committee consists of competent judges of men, it will select the candidate, *not for his potential wisdom as a legislator, but on his presumed ability to win elections!*

In a political party competence in one rank is a requisite for promotion to the next.

The Big Step: Candidate to Legislator

In bygone days, when great public meetings decided the results of elections, and when public speaking was a high art, a spellbinding orator might hope for nomination by a party, and the best orator among the candidates might win the seat. But of course the ability to charm, to amuse, to inflame a crowd of ten thousand voters with voice and gesture did not necessarily carry with it the ability to think sensibly, to debate soberly and to vote wisely on the nation's business.

With the development of electronic campaigning a party may give its nomination to the man who looks best on TV.

But the ability to impress—with the aid of makeup and lighting—an attractive image on a fluorescent screen is no guarantee of competent performance in the legislature.

Many a man, under the old and the new systems, has made the upward step from candidate to legislator, only to achieve his level of incompetence.

Incompetence in the Legislature

The legislature itself is a hierarchy. An elected representative who proves incompetent as a rank-and-file member will obtain no promotion.

But a competent rank-and-file legislator is eligible for promotion to a position of greater power—member of an important committee, committee chairman or, under some systems, cabinet minister. At any of these ranks, too, the promotee may be incompetent.

So we see that the Peter Principle controls the entire legislative arm of government, from the humblest party worker to the holders of the loftiest elective offices. Each tends to rise to his level and each post tends in time to be occupied by someone incompetent to carry out its duties.

The Executive

It will be obvious to you by now that the Principle applies also to the executive branch: government bureaus, departments, agencies and offices at the national, regional and local level. All, from police forces to armed forces, are rigid hierarchies of salaried employees, and all are necessarily cumbered with incompetents who cannot do their existing work, cannot be promoted, yet cannot be removed.

Any government, whether it is a democracy, a dictatorship, a communistic or free enterprise bureaucracy, will fall when its hierarchy reaches an intolerable state of maturity.*

Equalitarianism and Incompetence

The situation is worse than it used to be when civil service and military appointments were made through favoritism. This may sound heretical in an age of equalitarianism but allow me to explain.

Consider an imaginary country called Pullovia, where civil service examinations, equality of opportunity and promotion by merit are unknown. Pullovia has a rigid class system, and the high ranks in all hierarchies—government, business, the armed forces, the church—are reserved for members of the dominant class.

You will notice that I avoid the expression "upper class"; that term has unfortunate connotations. It is generally considered to refer to a class which is dominant by reason of aristocratic or genteel birth. But my conclusions apply also to systems in which the dominant class is marked off from the subordinate class by differences of religion, stature, race, language, dialect or political affiliation.

It does not matter which of these is the criterion in Pullovia: the important fact is that the country has a dominant class and a subordinate class. This diagram represents

---

* The efficiency of a hierarchy is inversely proportional to its Maturity Quotient, M.Q.

$$MQ = \frac{\text{No. of employees at level of incompetence} \times 100}{\text{Total no. of employees in hierarchy}}$$

Obviously, when MQ reaches 100, no useful work will be accomplished at all.

a typical Pullovian hierarchy which has the classical pyramidal structure.

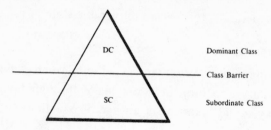

The lower ranks—the area marked SC—are occupied by employees of the subordinate class. No matter how brilliant any of them may be, no one is eligible to rise above CB, the class barrier.

The higher ranks—the area marked DC—are occupied by dominant-class employees. They do not start their careers at the bottom of the hierarchy, but at the level of the class barrier.

Now, in the lower area, SC, it is obvious that many employees will never be able to rise high enough, because of the class barrier, to reach their level of incompetence. They will spend their whole careers working at tasks which they are able to do well. No one is promoted out of area SC, so this area keeps, and continually utilizes, its competent employees.

Obviously, then, in the lower ranks of a hierarchy, the maintenance of a class barrier ensures a higher degree of efficiency than could possibly exist without the barrier.

Now look at area DC, above the class barrier. As we have already seen, an employee's prospects of reaching his level of incompetence are directly proportional to the number of ranks in the hierarchy—the more ranks, the more incompetence. The area DC, for all practical purposes, forms a closed hierarchy of a few ranks. Obviously, then, many of its employees will never reach their level of incompetence.

Moreover, the prospect of starting near the top of the pyramid will attract to the hierarchy a group of brilliant employees who would never have come there at all if they had been forced to start at the bottom.

Look at the situation another way. In Chapter 9 I shall discuss efficiency surveys, and shall show that the only effective way of increasing efficiency in a hierarchy is by the infusion of new blood at its upper levels. In most present-day systems, such infusion takes place at intervals, say after a reorganization, or during periods of rapid expansion. But in Pullovian hierarchies, it is a continuous process: new employees are regularly entering at a high level, above the class barrier.

Obviously, then, in areas SC and DC, below and above the class barrier, Pullovian hierarchies are more efficient than those of a classless or equalitarian society.

A Contemporary Class System

Before I am accused of recommending the establishment of a class system here, let me point out that we already have one. Its classes are based, not on birth, but on the prestige of the university which one has attended. For example, a graduate of Harvard is referred to as "A Harvard Man" but a graduate of Outer Sheepskin College is not referred to as "A Sheepskin Man." In some hierarchies, the graduate of the obscure college—no matter how competent he may be— does not have the same opportunities for promotion as the graduate of the prestigious establishment.

The situation is changing. There is a strong trend toward

making university graduation a prerequisite for more and more positions, even in the lowest ranks of certain hierarchies. This should increase the promotion potential of all degree holders, and therefore diminish the class value of the prestige degree.

My personal studies of this phenomenon are incomplete, due to that most lamentable dearth of funds, but I will hazard a prediction that with every passing year, each university graduate will have greater opportunities for reaching his level of incompetence, either in private employment, or in government.

He accurately observed the satisfaction that is obtained from doing one's work competently:

> *Know, all the good that individuals find,*
> *Or God and Nature meant to mere Mankind,*
> *Reason's whole pleasure, all the joys of Sense,*
> *Lie in three words, Health, Peace, and Competence.*
>
> <div align="right">(<i>Ibid.</i>, ll. 77–80)</div>

Pope enunciates one of the key principles of hierarchiology:

> *What would this man? Now upward will he soar,*
> *And little less than angel, would be more.*
>
> <div align="right">(Essay on Man, <i>Epistle I</i>, ll. 173–74)</div>

In other words, scarcely an employee is content to remain at his level of competence: he insists upon rising to a level that is beyond his powers.

S. Smith's description of occupational incompetence is so vivid that it has lingered on as the basis of a cliché.

> If you choose to represent the various parts in life by holes upon a table, of different shapes—some circular, some triangular, some square, some oblong—and the persons acting these parts by bits of wood of similar shapes, we shall generally find that the triangular person has got into the square hole, the oblong into the triangular, and a square person has squeezed himself into the round hole. The officer and the office, the doer and the thing done, seldom fit so easily that we can say they were almost made for each other.*

W. Irving points out that "Your true dull minds are generally preferred for public employ, and especially promoted to city honors." He did not realize that a mind may well be

---

* Smith, Sydney (1771–1845). *Sketches of Moral Philosophy*, 1850.

bright enough for a subordinate position, yet appear dull when promoted to prominence, just as a candle is all very well to light a dinner table, but proves inadequate if placed on a lamppost to illuminate a street corner.

K. Marx undoubtedly recognized the existence of hierarchies, yet seemed to believe that they were maintained by the capitalists. In advocating a non-hierarchal society, he obviously failed to see that man is essentially hierarchal by nature, and must and will have hierarchies, whether they be patriarchal, feudal, capitalistic or socialistic. On this point his insight is vastly inferior to that of Pope.

Then, with glaring inconsistency, Marx proposes, as the ruling principle of his non-hierarchal dream society, "From each according to his abilities and to each according to his needs." This suggests the creation of twin hierarchies of ability and neediness.

Even if we overlook this inconsistency in the Marxian scheme, the Peter Principle now shows that we cannot hope to obtain work "from each according to his ability." To do that, we should have to keep employees permanently at a level of competence. But that is impossible: each employee must rise to his level of incompetence and, once arrived at that level, will *not* be able to produce according to his ability.

So we see Marxist theory as a pipe dream and another opiate of the masses. No government which has tried to apply it has ever been able to make it work. Marx must be dismissed as an unscientific visionary.

We seem to find better science among the poets. E. Dickinson's aphorism

> *Success is counted sweetest*
> *By those who ne'er succeed*

is psychologically sound when "success" receives its hierarchiological meaning of final placement at the level of incompetence.

C. W. Dodgson, in *Through the Looking-Glass,* refers to life at the level of incompetence when he makes the Queen say, "Now *here,* you see, it takes all the running you can do to keep in the same place." In other words, once an employee has achieved final placement, his most vigorous efforts will never win him any further promotion.

S. Freud seems to have come closer than any earlier writer to discovering the Peter Principle. Observing cases of neurosis, anxiety, psychosomatic illness, amnesia, and psychosis, he saw the painful prevalence of what we might call the Generalized Life-Incompetence Syndrome.

This life-incompetence naturally produces sharp feelings of frustration. Freud, a satirist at heart, chose to explain this frustration mainly in sexual terms such as penis envy, castration complex and Oedipus complex. In other words, he suggested that women were frustrated because they could not be men, men because they could not bear children, boys because they could not marry their mothers and so on.

But Freud missed the point in thinking that frustration comes from the longing for a change to a more desirable position (man, father, mother's husband, father's wife, etc.), in other words, a longing for a promotion! Hierarchiology now shows us, of course, that frustration occurs as a result of promotion.

This oversight of Freud's occurred because of his extremely introspective nature: he persisted in studying what was going on (or what he imagined was going on) inside his patients. Hierarchiology, on the other hand, studies what is going on *outside* the patient, studies the social order in which man operates, and therefore realistically explains man's function in that order. While Freud spent his time hunting in the dark recesses of the subconscious, I have devoted my efforts to examining observable and measurable human behavior.

Freudian psychologists, in their failure to study the function of man in society, might be compared with a man seeing an electronic computer and trying to understand it by speculating on the internal structure and mechanism without trying to find out what the instrument was used for.

Still, let us not minimize Freud's pioneering work. Although he misunderstood much, he discovered much. Always looking within the patient, he became famous on the strength of his theory that man is unconscious of his own motivations, does not understand his own feelings and so cannot hope to relieve his own frustrations. The theory was unassailable, because nobody could consciously and rationally argue about the nature and contents of his unconscious.

With a stroke of professional genius he invented psychoanalysis, whereby he said he could make patients conscious of their unconscious.

Then he went too far, psychoanalyzed himself and claimed to be conscious of his own unconscious. (Some critics now suggest that all he had ever accomplished was to make *his patients* aware of *his own*—Freud's—unconscious.) In any event, by this procedure of self-psychoanalysis he kicked the ladder from under his own feet.

If Freud had understood hierarchiology, he would have shunned that last step, and would never have arrived at his level of incompetence.

By thus undermining the grand structure, which he had

built on the impenetrability of the unconscious, Freud prepared the way for his great successor, S. Potter.

Potter, like Freud, is a satirical psychologist (or a psychological satirist), and he can fairly be ranked with Freud for keenness of observation and boldness in creating a picturesque and memorable terminology to describe what he saw.

Like Freud, Potter observed and classified many phenomena of human frustration. The basic condition of being frustrated he calls being "one-down," and the exhilarated feeling caused by removal of frustration he calls "one-up." He assumes that men have an innate urge to advance from the former state to the latter. The technique for making this move he calls "one-upmanship."

The main difference between the two men is that Potter rejects Freud's doctrine of unconscious motivation. He explains human behavior in terms of a conscious drive to outdo other people, triumph over circumstances, and so become one-up. Potter also repudiates Freudian dogma that the frustrated patient must receive professional aid, and expounds a do-it-yourself brand of psychology. He teaches various plots, ploys and gambits that, if properly used, will enable the patient to become one-up.

The One-upman, the Lifeman, the Gamesman, to summarize Potter's elegantly expressed theories, are all using various forms of obnoxious behavior to move themselves up the ranks of social, commercial, professional or sporting hierarchies.

Potter writes so entertainingly that we tend to overlook the central weakness of his system, the assumption that, if only the One-upman can learn enough ploys, he can keep on rising, and can be permanently one-up.

In reality, no amount of One-upmanship can raise a man

above his level of incompetence. The only result of the technique will be to help him reach that level sooner than he would have done otherwise. And, once there, he is in a one-down situation which no amount of lifemanship can cure.

Lasting happiness is obtainable only by avoiding the ultimate promotion, by choosing, at a certain point in one's progress, to abandon one-upmanship, and to practice instead what he might have called *Staticmanship*. I shall point out later, in the chapter on Creative Incompetence, how this can be done.

Meanwhile, I must salute Potter as a truly great theoretician who ably bridged the gap between the Freudian Ethic and the Peter Principle.

No amount of One-upmanship can raise a man above his level of incompetence.

C. N. Parkinson, eminent social theorist, accurately observes and amusingly describes the phenomenon of staff accumulation in hierarchies. But he tries to explain what he calls the rising pyramid by supposing that senior employees are practicing the strategy of divide and conquer, that they are deliberately making the hierarchy inefficient as a means of self-aggrandizement.

This theory fails on the following grounds. First, it assumes intent or design on the part of persons in supervisory positions. My investigations show that many senior employees are incapable of formulating any effective plans, for division, conquest or any other purpose.

Second, the phenomena that Parkinson describes—overstaffing and underproduction—are often directly opposed to the interests of the supervisory and managerial personnel. Efficiency becomes so low that businesses collapse, and the responsible employees find themselves out of work. In governmental hierarchies they may be badgered and humiliated by legislative committees, or commissioners, investigating waste and incompetence. It is scarcely conceivable that they would deliberately injure themselves in this way.

Third, other things being equal, the less money that is spent on the wages of subordinates, the larger will be the profits of the business, and the more money will be available for salaries, bonuses, dividends and fringe benefits for the high-ranking staff. If the hierarchy can function efficiently with a thousand employees, management has no motive for employing twelve hundred.

But suppose the hierarchy is not operating efficiently with its thousand employees. As the Peter Principle shows, many, or most, senior employees will be at their levels of incompetence. They cannot do anything to improve the situation with their existing staff—everyone is already doing the best he can—so in a desperate effort to attain efficiency, they hire more staff. As pointed out in Chapter 3, a staff increase may produce a temporary improvement, but the promotion process eventually produces its effect on the newcomers and they, too, rise to their levels of incompetence. Then the only apparent remedy is another staff increase, another temporary spurt and another gradual lapse into inefficiency.

This is the reason why there is no direct relationship between the size of the staff and the amount of useful work done. Staff accumulation cannot be explained by Parkinson's conspiracy theory: it results from a sincere, though futile, quest for efficiency by upper-level members of the hierarchy.

Another point: Parkinson based his law on the Cheopsian or feudal hierarchy.

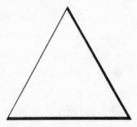

The Cheopsian or Feudal Hierarchy

The reason for this is that Parkinson made his discovery in the armed forces, where obsolete traditions and modes of organization have the strongest foothold.

To be sure, the feudal hierarchy has not disappeared, but a complete hierarchiological system must also recognize the existence and explain the operations of several other hierarchal forms.

For example, the *Flying T Formation*

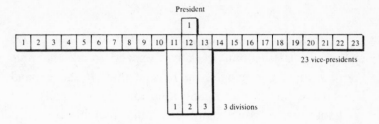

This diagram clearly illustrates that a company with 3 major divisions, 23 vice-presidents and 1 president does not fit the traditional pyramidal model.

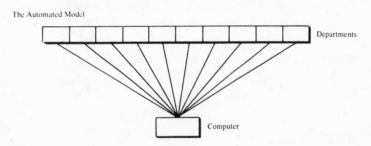

In this recent modification the broad pyramidal base of employees is replaced by a computer.

Many departments are supported by one computer, producing an inverted pyramid. A similar form results when numerous executive, supervisory and sales staff are supported by a highly automated production process.

I have already described, in Chapter 3, the Free-Floating Apex—a condition which exists when a director is in charge of a non-existent department, or when a staff is assigned to another department leaving the administrator to his lonely office.

⋀ Administrator

Free-Floating Apex

Unfortunately Parkinson's investigation does not go far enough. It is true that work can expand to fill the time allotted but it can expand far beyond that. It can expand beyond the life of the organization and the company can go bankrupt, a government can fall, a civilization can crumble into barbarism, while the incompetents work on. We must therefore regretfully dismiss Parkinson's attractive-sounding theory. Nevertheless, great praise is due to him for drawing attention to those phenomena which are now, for the first time, scientifically explained by the Peter Principle.

CHAPTER IX

The Psychology of Hierarchiology

"Alas! regardless of their doom
The little victims play."

T. GRAY

AFTER one of my hierarchiology lectures a student handed me a note which included the following questions. "Why did you not give us some insight into the mind of the incompetent loafer type you described so vividly? After final placement, does the employee realize his own incompetence? Does he accept his own parasitism? Does he know that he is swindling his employer, frustrating his subordinates, and eating like a cancer at the economic structure of society?" Recently I have received many questions of this type.

A Dispassionate Survey

I must first emphasize that *hierarchiology is a social science* and as such employs objective criteria in its evaluation rather than emotion-laden terms like "loafer," "parasite,"

91

"swindling" or "cancer." The question of insight, though, is worthy of consideration. My approach to behavioral science has been that of an objective observer. I discovered the Peter Principle through observing overt behavior and have avoided introspection or inferences regarding what is going on in the minds of others.

Mirror, Mirror, on the Wall

Yet the question of insight is, in essence, an interesting one: "What understanding does the individual attain into his own copelessness?" My answers to this question are subjective and lack the scientific rigor of the balance of this work.

In most cases I have found little indication of real insight. However, a few cases in my study were in analysis, and I was able to obtain psychiatric reports. These showed that patients rationalized and blamed other people for their difficulties.

Where depth analysis was achieved, there was more acceptance of self. Yet I never observed, in an individual, any understanding of the hierarchal system, or of *promotion as the cause of occupational incompetence.*

PSYCHIATRIC FILE: CASE NO. 12   S. N. Stickle was a competent stock clerk with Bathos Brothers Lead Weight and Sinker Company. By hard night-school study, Stickle gained diplomas in warehouse management and elementary non-ferrous metallurgy. He was promoted to assistant warehouse foreman.

After six years in this post, Stickle asked for another promotion. He was told that he lacked leadership ability: he could not make the warehousemen obey his commands; so he was not eligible for promotion to warehouse foreman.

But Stickle could not accept the truth about his own incompetence as a supervisor. He rationalized that the big, burly warehousemen scorned him because he was only five feet six inches tall.

He bought elevator shoes, and took to wearing a hat in the warehouse; this made him look taller. He attended a body-building studio, gained weight and developed bulging muscles. Still the warehousemen did not obey him.

Stickle brooded over his physical deficiencies, developed a severe complex, and eventually sought psychiatric advice.

During therapy Dr. Harty tried to help Stickle by telling him about small men who had achieved fame and fortune. This made Stickle more depressed: now he saw himself not only as small, but as an obscure failure. His self-confidence deteriorated further, and he became still less competent as a supervisor.

He saw himself not only as small, but as an obscure failure.

Psychiatry, Like Love, Is Not Enough

The Stickle case shows that, without an understanding of the Peter Principle, psychiatry is at a severe disadvantage in trying to treat problems arising from occupational incompetence.

Dr. Harty was diverted by an irrelevancy, Stickle's stature. Stickle's situation was simply that, within the Bathos Brothers' hierarchy, he had reached his level of incompetence. No psychiatric treatment could alter that fact.

But Stickle might have been consoled had he been shown that his coming to rest in the position of assistant warehouse foreman was *not failure, but fulfillment.*

He might have been happier had he realized that his was not a solitary example of misfortune, but that everyone else, in every hierarchal system was, like him, under the sway of the Peter Principle.

I do feel that an understanding of the principle will aid the analysis of all cases exhibiting any degree of copelessness.

Insight Is Not Enough, Either!

Sometimes, after granting a promotion, *management attains insight* and realizes that the promotee cannot properly fulfill his new responsibilities.

"Grindley *isn't working out too well* as foreman."

"Goode *wasn't quite big enough,* after all, to fill Betters' shoes."

"Miss Cardington *isn't shaping up* as filing supervisor."

Occasionally *the employee* also attains this insight and accepts his own incompetence for the higher rank. Here, too, insight produces much regretful thought, but little or no action.

INSIGHT FILE, CASE NO. 2   F. Overreach, a competent school vice-principal in Excelsior City, was promoted to principal. Before one term was over, he realized that he was incompetent for the job.

He asked to be demoted. His application was refused!

He remains, unhappy and resentful, at his level of incompetence.

Outside Investigators

I mentioned that management and employees do sometimes achieve insight into occupational incompetence but do little to counteract it. You may now be thinking, "But what about vocational aptitude tests? What about efficiency surveys? Surely disinterested outside observers can diagnose incompetence and can prescribe appropriate remedies."

Can they? Let us look at these experts and see how they run.

Placement Methods, Old-fashioned and Newfangled

In olden days, entry into most careers was governed by random placement, based on the employer's prejudices, on the employee's wishes or on chance (an applicant happens to turn up seeking work just at the moment when a vacancy occurs). Random placement is still operative in some hierarchies, particularly the smaller ones.

Random placement often puts an employee into a position that he is barely competent to fill. His mediocre work is blamed on a vicious character, flabby will-power or plain laziness. He is exhorted to work harder. He is edified with such adages as "Where there's a will, there's a way," and "If at first you don't succeed, try, try again."

In bad favor with his superiors, his first promotion is long delayed. (He may even come to believe that he is worthless, undeserving of any advancement at all: I call this condition *The Uriah Heep Syndrome*.)

Random placement is now largely superseded by examinations and aptitude tests. The prevailing attitude is best expressed in the saying, "If at first you don't succeed, try something else."

Of course, it is no use giving aptitude tests if you have no competent person to mark the papers and interpret the scores. With incompetent handling, the test system is only a disguised form of random placement.

But, if competently handled, aptitude tests have their uses. We have general aptitude or intelligence tests, which sample ability with language, ingenuity, computational facility and so on. There are clerical tests which indicate skill in remembering numbers, copying names and addresses and so forth. There are tests which rate a person for mechanical ability, artistic ability, physical skill, social intelligence, scientific reasoning and persuasiveness.

Test results are commonly expressed in a "profile," a graphic representation of the employee's competence in various skills. Here is such a profile.

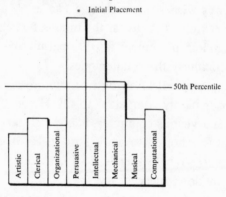

The purpose of this testing is to place the employee, as soon as possible, in a job which will utilize the highest competence level on his profile. Obviously, *any promotion will be to an area of less competence*.

Let us see how this works in practice.

PLACEMENT TECHNIQUES FILE, CASE NO. 17 The profile shown above actually resulted from the testing of C. Breeze, a young commerce graduate, who applied for a post with the I. C. Gale Air Conditioning Company. You will notice that Breeze is above average in persuasive ability, and also has high general intelligence.

Breeze was hired as a salesman and in time achieved two promotions: first to District Sales Manager, where he still spent much of his time selling, and then to General Sales Manager, a supervisory and organizational post.

Note that his lowest score, much below average, is in organizational ability. This is the very faculty that he now uses daily. For example, his salesmen are assigned arbitrarily. Hap Hazard, an inexperienced salesman, was sent to call on two new important clients and managed to lose both sales and goodwill. Conn Manly, a new employee who had achieved an impressive sales record, was promoted to district sales manager. He showed little sincere interest in his salesmen. His calculated, crafty methods of manipulation have reduced morale of his men to a new low.

C. Breeze also mismanaged paperwork. The size and topography of sales territories had no relationship to transportation, volume of business or salesmen's experience and ability. His memos and records are beyond comprehension and his desk looks like a litter pile.

As the Peter Principle predicts, his career has proceeded from competence to incompetence.

Aptitude Testing Evaluated

The main difference between tested and untested employees is that the tested people reach their levels of incompetence in fewer steps and in a shorter time.

Efficiency Surveys

We have seen that outside intervention at the time of initial placement cannot prevent but in fact hastens achievement of incompetence levels. I will now examine the operations of efficiency experts who, of course, usually appear on the scene at a later stage, when a hierarchy has achieved a high Maturity Quotient. (M.Q. defined, Chapter 7.)

First, we must remember that the investigating experts, too, are subject to the Peter Principle. They have reached their position by the same promotion process that has crippled the organization they are surveying. Many of the experts will be at their level of incompetence. Even if they can see deficiencies, they will be unable to correct them.

EFFICIENCY SURVEY FILE, CASE NO. 8 Bulkeley Cold Store and Transfer Ltd. hired Speedwell and Trimmer, Management Consultants, to survey its operation. Speedwell and Trimmer found that the Bulkeley organization was no more inefficient than most firms in the same line of business. By discreet questioning they discovered the real reason why the survey had been ordered: several directors felt that they could not sufficiently influence the firm's policy.

What could Speedwell and Trimmer do? Suppose they

said, "Gentlemen, there is not much wrong with your firm. You are as efficient as your competitors."

There is good reason to believe that Speedwell and Trimmer fear dismissal in such an instance. They may feel they would get the reputation of being inefficient management experts; they would see the Bulkeley survey taken over by a rival firm.

Under this emotional stress they felt obliged to say, "Gentlemen, you are understaffed, and many of your existing employees are wrongly placed. We recommend the creation of certain new posts, and the promotion of a number of your employees."

Once the organization was thoroughly stirred up, the dissident directors could place or promote protégés just as they wished, thereby strengthening their influence at various levels and in various departments of the hierarchy. The board was satisfied, and Speedwell and Trimmer received their fee.

Management Surveys Evaluated

1) An efficiency survey, in effect, temporarily weakens, or even suspends, the operation of the Seniority Factor in a hierarchy. This automatically hastens promotion, or facilitates initial placement, for employees who have Pull (Pullees).

2) A favorite recommendation of efficiency experts is the appointment of *a co-ordinator between two incompetent officials or two unproductive departments.** A popular fal-

---

* A survey of efficiency experts reveals that co-ordinator appointments, lateral arabesques and percussive sublimations are always acceptable to management.

lacy among these experts and their clients is that "Incompetence co-ordinated equals competence."

3) *The only recommendation* that actually produces an increase of output is "Hire more employees." In some instances, new recruits will do work which is not being done by the old employees who have reached their level.

The effective management consultant realizes this and recommends various lateral arabesques and percussive sublimations of high-ranking incompetents and hierarchal exfoliation of super-incompetent low-ranking employees. Competent consultants also make useful recommendations regarding personnel practices, production methods, color dynamics, incentive schemes and so forth, which can improve the efficiency of the competent employees.

Compulsive Incompetence

While reviewing depth studies of a few cases of competence at the top levels of hierarchies, a remarkable psychological phenomenon presented itself to me and I will here describe it.

Summit Competence is rare, but not completely unknown. In Chapter 1, I wrote, "Given enough time—and assuming the existence of enough ranks in the hierarchy—each employee rises to, and remains at, his level of incompetence."

Victorious field marshals, successful school superintendents, competent company presidents and such persons have simply not *had time* to reach their levels of incompetence.

Alternatively, the emergence of a competent trade-union leader or university president simply shows that, *in that par-*

ticular hierarchy, there are not enough ranks for him to reach his level.

These people exhibit *Summit Competence.**

I have observed that these summit competents are often not satisfied to remain in their position of competence. They cannot rise to a position of incompetence—they are already at the top—*so they have a strong tendency to sidestep into another hierarchy*—say from the army into industry, from politics into education, from show business into politics and so on—*and reach, in the new environment, that level of incompetence which they could not find in the old.* This is *Compulsive Incompetence.*

Compulsive Incompetence File, Selected Cases

Macbeth, a successful military commander, became an incompetent king.

A. Hitler, a consummate politician, found his level of incompetence as a generalissimo.

Socrates was an incomparable teacher, but found his level of incompetence as a defense attorney.

Why Do They Do It?

"The job lacks challenge."

This, or some variant of it, is the reason invariably given

---

* Our records contain a few outstanding cases of *Multi-modal Summit Competence*—individuals who could be at the summit of several hierarchies at one time. A. Einstein is an example of this phenomenon. He was a highly competent thinker who provided science with a special and general theory of relativity. It was also obvious that Einstein was highly competent in the area of men's fashions. His hair style and casual clothing established a trend followed by young people to this day. Considering what he accomplished in the fashion world without effort, one wonders what he might have achieved if he had really tried.

by summit competents at the time when they are considering the move which will eventually lead them to compulsive incompetence.

Need They Do It?

There is in fact a greater, more fascinating challenge in remaining below one's level of incompetence. I shall discuss that point in a later chapter.

CHAPTER X

Peter's Spiral

"We all of us live too much in a circle."
B. DISRAELI

I pointed out in Chapter 9 that hierarchiology is not moralistic with regard to incompetence. Indeed, I must say that, in most cases of incompetence, there appears to be a definite *wish to be productive*. The employee *would be competent if he could*.

Most incompetents realize, however dimly, that the collapse of the organization would leave them jobless, so they try to keep the hierarchy going.

Let me give an illustration.

Intra-Hierarchal File, Case No. 4

Health for Wealth

In twenty years at Perfect Pewter Piano Strings Inc., Mal D'Mahr had worked his way up from lead ingot handler to general manager. Shortly after occupying the chief executive office he suffered a series of health problems associated with high blood pressure and peptic ulcers. The company physician recommended that he slow down and learn to relax. The board of directors recommended that an assistant general manager be appointed to relieve Mal of some of the strain. Although both of these recommendations were well intentioned they failed to deal with the cause of the problem. Hierarchiologically Mal D'Mahr had been promoted beyond his physiological competence. As chief executive at P.P.P.S.I. he had to deal with and accommodate conflicting codes or values. He had to please the stockholders and board by making money. He had to please the customers by maintaining a high-quality product. He had to please the employees by paying good wages and by providing comfortable, secure working conditions. He had to please his community by fulfilling certain social and family responsibilities. In attempting to accommodate these conflicting codes he broke down physically. No increase in staff or advice about relaxing could reduce this requirement of the office of the chief executive.

Calculate the Unknown

The board's recommendation was carried out and J. Smugly, a competent engineer and mathematical genius, was promoted to assistant general manager. Smugly, competent in dealing with things, was incompetent at dealing with people. He had no appropriate people-formulas to help him decide about personnel matters. Not wishing to act on incomplete data, he postponed personnel decisions until pressure became so great that he made unwise, snap decisions. Smugly reached his level of incompetence through social inadequacy. It was recommended that he be assisted through the appointment of a personnel manager.

In attempting to accommodate these conflicting codes he broke down physically.

Compassion Is Its Own Reward

Roly Koster was promoted to the position of personnel manager. A competent psychology student, he soon became so empathetic with his clients that he was perpetually on an emotional binge. When he listened to Smugly's complaint about an inaccurate report from Miss Count, his sympathy was with the assistant general manager and he was filled with anger toward Miss Count for her carelessness. When he heard Miss Count's story about Smugly's cold, calculating, inhuman approach toward her and her colleagues he was brought to tears of sorrow and indignation at Smugly's heartlessness. Roly achieved his level of incompetence through emotional inadequacy. To resolve some of the personnel problems it was decided to create a new position of personnel supervisor and to promote someone from the plant who had the confidence of the men.

Mind Over Matter

B. Willder was popular with the men and had distinguished himself as chairman of the social committee. Now as personnel supervisor he is required to see that the policy decisions of management are carried out. But, as he does not really understand the policy, B. Willder is ineffective in this role. He lacks the intellectual capacity to deal effectively with abstraction and therefore makes illogical decisions. He has reached his level of incompetence through mental inadequacy.

Incompetence Classified

I have reported this study, conducted at Perfect Pewter Piano Strings Inc., because it illustrates the four basic classes of incompetence.

Mal D'Mahr was promoted beyond his *physical competence*.

J. Smugly was promoted beyond his *social competence*.

Roly Koster was promoted beyond his *emotional competence*.

B. Willder was promoted beyond his *mental competence*.

A Vain Effort

This example, typical of many, shows that even a sincere attempt to relieve high-level incompetence may only produce multi-level incompetence. In such circumstances, staff accumulation is inevitable. Each time around *Peter's Spiral*, the number of incompetents increases, and *still there is no improvement of efficiency.*

The Mathematics of Incompetence

Incompetence plus incompetence equals incompetence.

CHAPTER XI

The Pathology of Success

"Troubles never come singly."

———————

I T should be clear by now that when an employee reaches his level of incompetence, he can no longer do any useful work.

Incompetent, Yes! Idle, No!

This in no way suggests that the ultimate promotion suddenly changes the former worker into an idler. Not at all! In most cases he still *wants to work;* he still makes a great show of activity; he sometimes thinks he is working. Yet actually little that is useful is accomplished.

Sooner or later (usually sooner) these employees become aware of, and feel distressed at, their own unproductivity.

A Bold Step

Here we must venture into the field of medicine! I will describe the physical condition which has been alluded to earlier as the Final Placement Syndrome.

An Exhaustive Research Program

A number of medical doctors in general practice were asked:

1) "What physical conditions, if any, do you find to be most commonly associated with success?" *

2) "What advice or treatment, if any, do you give to patients in the success-group?"

An Alarming Report (1)

On collating the doctors' replies, I found that the following complaints from A to Z were common among their "successful" patients.

a) Peptic ulcers

b) Spastic colitis

c) Mucous colitis

d) High blood pressure

e) Constipation

f) Diarrhea

g) Frequent urination

h) Alcoholism

i) Overeating and obesity

j) Loss of appetite

k) Allergies

l) Hypertension

m) Muscle spasms

n) Insomnia

o) Chronic fatigue

p) Skipped heartbeats

q) Other cardiovascular complaints

r) Migraine headaches

s) Nausea and vomiting

t) Tender, painful abdomen

u) Dizziness

v) Dysmenorrhea

w) Tinnitus (ringing in the ears)

x) Excessive sweating of hands, feet, armpits or other areas

y) Nervous dermatitis

z) Sexual impotence

---

* What the ordinary sociologist or physician calls "success," the hierarchiologist, of course, recognizes as *final placement*.

All of these are typical "success" complaints, and may occur without the existence of organic disease.

I saw—and by now you will be able to see—that such symptoms indicate the constitutional incompetence of the patients for the level of responsibility they have attained.

A Case Study in Depth   For example, T. Throbmore, vice-president in charge of sales of Clacklow Office Machine Company, is frequently prevented from attending the company's weekly executive meeting by a migraine headache that occurs fairly regularly on Monday afternoons at 1:30 P.M.

Depth Study of Another Case   Because of the delicate condition of his heart, C. R. Diack, president of Grindley Gear and Cog Ltd., is permanently shielded by his staff from any news that might excite or irritate him. He has no real control over the company's affairs. His main function is to read glowing reports of its progress at annual meetings.

Note This Important Definition   The ailments I have named, usually occurring in combinations of two or more, constitute the Final Placement Syndrome.*

An Alarming Report (2)

Unfortunately, the medical profession has so far failed to recognize the existence of the Final Placement Syndrome! In fact, that profession has displayed a frigid hostility to-

---

* Refer to Chapter 5 for an infallible means of distinguishing the Final Placement Syndrome from the Pseudo-Achievement Syndrome.

ward my application of hierarchiology to the pseudo-science of diagnostics. However, truth will out! Time and the increasingly tumultuous social order inevitably will bring enlightenment.

Three Medical Errors (*a*)

Final Placement Syndrome patients often rationalize the situation: they claim that their occupational incompetence is the result of their physical ailments. "If only I could get rid of these headaches, I could concentrate on my work."

Or "If only I could get my digestion fixed up . . ."

Or "If I could kick the booze . . ."

Or "If I could get just one good night's sleep . . ."

Some medical men, my survey reveals, accept this rationalization at face value, and attack the physical symptoms without any search for their cause.

This attack is made by medication or surgery, either of which may give temporary, *but only temporary, relief.* The patient cannot be drugged into competence and there is no tumor of incompetence which can be removed by a stroke of the scalpel. *Good advice* is equally ineffective.

"Take it easy."

"Don't work so hard."

"Learn to relax."

Such soothing suggestions are useless. Many F.P.S. patients feel anxious because they know quite well that they are doing very little useful work. They are unlikely to follow any suggestion that they should do still less.

Another futile approach is that of *the friendly philosopher:*

"Stop trying to solve all the world's problems."

"Everybody has troubles. You're no worse off than lots of other people."

"You have to expect some of these problems at your age."

Few F.P.S. patients are susceptible to such cracker-barrel wisdom. Most of them are quite self-centered: they show little interest in philosophy or in other people's problems. They are only trying to solve the problems of their jobs.

Threats are often employed:

"If you carry on like this, you will end up in the hospital."

"Unless you slow down, you're going to have a really serious attack."

This is futile. The patient cannot help but "carry on like this." The only thing that would change his way of life would be a promotion, and he will not get that, because he has reached his level.

Another much-used line of advice is the *exhortation to self-denial.*

"Go on a diet."

"Cut down on your drinking."

"Stop smoking."

"Give up night life."

"Curb your sex life."

This is usually ineffective. The F.P.S. patient is already depressed because he can take no pleasure in his work. Why should he give up the few pleasures he has outside of work?

Moreover, many men feel that there is a certain aura of competence associated with heavy indulgence in bodily pleasures. It is reflected in such phrases as "He has a *wonderful* appetite," "He's a *great* ladies' man," and "He can hold his liquor." Such praise is doubly sweet to the man who has little else to be praised for; he will be reluctant to give it up.

Three Medical Errors (*b*)

A second group of physicians, finding nothing organically wrong with an F.P.S. patient, will try to persuade him that *his symptoms do not exist!*

"There's really nothing wrong with you. Just take these tranquillizers."

"Get your mind off yourself. These symptoms are only imaginary. It's your nerves."

Such advice, of course, produces no lasting improvement. The patient *knows that he is suffering,* whether the physician will admit it or not.

A common result is that the patient loses faith in the physician, and runs to another one, seeking someone who "understands his case" better. He may lose faith altogether in orthodox medicine and start consulting pseudo-medical practitioners.

Three Medical Errors (*c*)

After medication and surgery have failed, psychotherapy is sometimes tried. It seldom succeeds, because it can have no effect on the root cause of the F.P.S., which is the patient's vocational incompetence.

A Smattering of Sense

The only treatment, my survey shows, which gives any relief for the F.P.S. is distraction therapy.

"Learn to play bridge."

"Start a stamp collection."

"Take up gardening."

"Learn barbecue cookery."

"Paint pictures by numbers."

Typically, the doctor senses the patient's copelessness
with regard to his job, and so tries to divert his attention to
something that he can cope with.

AN ILLUMINATING CASE HISTORY W. Lushmoor, a de-
partment-store executive, spent every afternoon at his club,
rather than return to his office. An advanced F.P.S. case,
Lushmoor was a near-alcoholic, had survived two mild
coronary attacks, was grossly overweight and chronically
dyspeptic.

On his physician's advice, he took up golf. He became
obsessed by the game, devoted all his afternoons and most
of his energy to it, and was making rapid progress until he

W. Lushmoor spent every afternoon at his club.

suffered a fatal stroke while driving his electric golf cart.

The point is that, although Lushmoor's symptoms were not relieved, he had been transformed from an F.P.S. case in relation to his job—since he no longer worried about the job—to a mere Pseudo-Achievement Syndrome case in relation to golf! The treatment was therefore successful.

Physicians who give this sort of advice do seem to understand, even though dimly, the pathogenic role of incompetence; they try to give the patient a feeling of competence in some non-occupational field.

A Sinister Sign

One more point about the Final Placement Syndrome: it has an ever-increasing sociological importance, because its component ailments have acquired high status value. An F.P.S. patient will boast of his symptoms; he will show a perverse kind of competence in developing a bigger ulcer or a more severe heart attack than any of his friends. In fact, so high is the status value of the F.P.S. that some employees who have none of its ailments will actually simulate them, to create the impression that they have achieved final placement.

CHAPTER XII

Non-Medical Indices of Final Placement

"How can I tell the signals and the signs?"
H. W. Longfellow

A Long-Felt Want

It is often useful to know who, in a hierarchy, has and has not achieved final placement. Unfortunately, you cannot always get hold of an employee's medical record to see whether he is a Final Placement Syndrome case or not. So here are some signs which will guide you.

Abnormal Tabulology

This is an important and significant branch of hierarchiology.

The competent employee normally keeps on his desk just the books, papers and apparatus that he needs for his work.

After final placement, an employee is likely to adopt some unusual and highly significant arrangement of his desk.

Phonophilia

The employee rationalizes his incompetence by complaining that he cannot keep in close enough touch with colleagues and subordinates. To remedy this, he installs several telephones on his desk, one or more intercommunication devices with buttons, flashing lights and loudspeakers, plus one or more voice-recording machines. The phonophiliac soon forms the habit of using two or more of these devices at the same time; this is an infallible sign of galloping phonophilia. Such cases degenerate rapidly and are usually considered incurable.

(Phonophilia, by the way, is nowadays increasingly seen among women who have reached their level of incompetence as housewives. Typically, an elaborate microphone-loud-speaker-switchboard-telephone system is installed in the kitchen to enable such a housewife to keep in constant, close, simultaneous contact with her neighbors, her dining nook, her laundry room, her play room, her back porch and her mother.)

Papyrophobia

The papyrophobe cannot tolerate papers or books on his desk or, in extreme cases, anywhere in his office. Probably every such piece of paper is a reminder to him of the work that he is not able to do: no wonder he hates the sight of it!

But he makes a virtue out of his phobia and, by "keeping a clean desk," as he calls it, hopes to create the impression that he despatches all his business with incredible promptitude.

Papyromania

Papyromania, the exact opposite of papyrophobia, causes the employee to clutter his desk with piles of never-used papers and books. Consciously or unconsciously, he thus tries to mask his incompetence by giving the impression that he has *too much to do*—more than any human being could accomplish.

Fileophilia

Here we see a mania for the precise arrangement and classification of papers, usually combined with a morbid fear of the loss of any document. By keeping himself so busy with rearranging and re-examining bygone business, the fileophiliac prevents other people—and prevents himself—from realizing that he is accomplishing little or nothing of current importance. His preoccupation with records fixes his vision on the past so that he backs reluctantly into the present.

Tabulatory Gigantism

An obsession with having a bigger desk than his colleagues.

Tabulophobia Privata

Complete exclusion of desks from the office. This symptom is observed only at the very highest hierarchal ranks.

Psychological Manifestations

In my researches I spent much time in waiting rooms, interviewing clients and colleagues as they left executive offices. In this way I discovered several interesting psychological manifestations of final placement.

Self-Pity

Many executive conferences consisted of the high-ranking employee telling hard-luck stories about his present condition.

"Nobody really appreciates me."

"Nobody co-operates with me."

"Nobody understands how the incessant pressure from above and the incurable incompetence below make it utterly impossible for me to do an adequate job and keep a clean desk."

This self-pity is usually combined with a strong tendency to reminisce about "good old days" when the complainant was working at a lower rank, at a level of competence.

This complex of emotions—sentimental self-pity, denigration of the present and irrational praise of the past— I call *the Auld Lang Syne Complex.*

An interesting feature of the Auld Lang Syne Complex is that although the typical patient claims to be a martyr to his present position, he never on any account suggests that another employee would be better able to fill his place!

Rigor Cartis

In employees at the level of incompetence, I have often observed Rigor Cartis, an abnormal interest in the construction of organization and flow charts, and a stubborn insistence upon routing every scrap of business in strict accordance wth the lines and arrows of the chart, no matter what delays or losses may result. The Rigor Cartis patient will often display his charts prominently on the office walls, and may sometimes be seen, his work lying neglected, standing in worshipful contemplation of his icons.

Compulsive Alternation

Some employees, on achieving final placement, try to mask their insecurity by keeping their subordinates always off balance.

An executive of this type is handed a written report; he pushes it aside and says, "I've no time to wade through all that garbage. Tell me about it in your own words—and briefly."

If the subordinate comes in with a verbal suggestion, this man chokes him off in mid-sentence with, "I can't even begin to think about it until you put it in writing."

A confident employee will be deflated with a snub; a timid one will be flustered by a display of familiarity. One may at first confuse Compulsive Alternation with Potter's One-upmanship but they are quite different. Potter's method is designed to advance the user to his level of incompetence. Compulsive Alternation is primarily a defensive technique employed by a boss who has reached his level.

This man's subordinates say, "You never know how to take him."

The Teeter-Totter Syndrome

In the teeter-totter syndrome one sees a complete inability to make the decisions appropriate to the sufferer's rank. An employee of this type can balance endlessly and minutely the pros and cons of a question, but cannot come down on one side or the other. He will rationalize his immobility with grave allusions to "the democratic process" or "taking the longer view." He usually deals with the problems that come to him by keeping them in limbo until someone else makes a decision or until it is too late for a solution.

I notice, by the way, that teeter-totter victims are often papyrophobes as well, so they have to find some means of getting rid of the papers. *The Downward, Upward and Outward Buckpasses* are commonly used to effect this.

In the Downward Buckpass the papers are sent to a subordinate with the order, "Don't bother me with such trifles." The subordinate is thus bullied into deciding an issue that is really above his level of responsibility.

The Upward Buckpass calls for ingenuity: the teeter-totter victim must examine the case until he finds some tiny point out of the ordinary which will justify sending it up to a higher level.

The Outward Buckpass merely involves assembling a committee of the victim's peers and following the decision of the majority. A variant of this is *The John Q. Public Diversion:* sending the papers to someone else who will conduct a survey to find what the average citizen thinks about the matter.

One teeter-totter victim in government service resolved his problem in an original manner. When he got a case that he could not decide, he would simply remove the file from the office at night and throw it away.

A Classical Case

W. Shakespeare describes an interesting manifestation of final placement: an irrational prejudice against subordinates or colleagues because of some point of physical appearance in no way related to the performance of their work. He quotes Julius Caesar as saying:

> *Let me have men about me that are fat. . . .*
> *Yon Cassius has a lean and hungry look;*
> *He thinks too much: such men are dangerous.*

It is reliably reported that N. Bonaparte, toward the end of his career, began judging men by the size of their noses, and would give preferment only to men with big noses.

Some victims of this obsession may attach their baseless dislikes to such trifles as the shape of a chin, a regional accent, the cut of a coat or the width of a necktie. Actual competence or incompetence on the job is ignored. This prejudice I call *The Caesarian Transference.*

Cachinatory Inertia

A sure mark of final placement is the habit of *telling jokes* instead of getting on with business!

A sure mark of final placement is the habit of telling jokes instead of getting on with business.

Structurophilia

Structurophilia is an obsessive concern with buildings—their planning, construction, maintenance and reconstruction—and an increasing unconcern with the work that is going on, or is supposed to be going on, inside them. I have observed structurophilia at all hierarchal levels, but it undoubtedly achieves its finest development in politicians and university presidents. In its extreme pathological manifestations (*Gargantuan monumentalis*) it reaches a stage where the victim has a compulsion to build great tombs or memorial statues. Ancient Egyptians and modern Southern Californians appear to have suffered greatly from this malady.

Structurophilia has been referred to, by the uninformed, as the Edifice Complex. We must be precise in differentiating between this simple preoccupation with structures and the Edifice Complex which involves a number of elaborately interrelated, interconnected and complicated attitudes. The Edifice Complex tends to afflict philanthropists wishing to improve education, health services or religious instruction. They consult experts in these fields and discover so many at their respective levels of incompetence that formulation of a positive program is impossible. The only thing they agree on is to have a new building. Frequently the advising educator, doctor or minister suffers from structurophilia and therefore his recommendation to the donor is, "Give me a new building." Church committees, school trustees and foundation boards find themselves in the same *complex* situation. They see so much incompetence in the professions that they decide to invest in buildings rather than people and programs. As in other psychological complexes, this results in bizarre behaviour.

RELIGIOUS PROGRAM IMPROVEMENT FILE #64   The congregational committee of the First Euphoria Church in Excelsior City became concerned with declining church attendance. Various proposals were investigated. One faction recommended a change of minister. They were tired of Reverend Theo Log's traditional sermons that had little to say about the contemporary human condition. As a result guest clergy were invited. Questions were raised regarding the sexual revolution, generation gap, the futility of war, and the new morality. Some of the more conservative church members threatened to quit if these "far-out" sermons continued. The committee finally agreed that a building drive and new church would be the most acceptable solution. The old minister was retained at his low salary. After completion of the new building it came to the committee's attention that the small congregation seemed even smaller in the large new church. The recommendation for a more dynamic ministry was reconsidered but was rejected because it was decided that it would be impossible to get a better man for such a low salary. Furthermore, it was concluded, this might seriously hamper the funding of the new organ and the building of the new social centre.

Which Is Which

Usually the structurophilia victim has a pathological need to have a building or monument named in his honor, whereas the Edifice Complex afflicts those who are trying to improve the quality of some human endeavor but end up by only producing another building.

Tics and Odd Habits

Eccentric physical habits and tics often develop soon after final placement has been achieved. A noteworthy example is *Heep's Palmar Confrication,* so acutely observed and vividly described by C. Dickens.

I would also mention under this head such habits as nail biting, drumming with fingers or tapping with pencils on desks, cracking knuckles, twiddling pens, pencils and paper clips, the purposeless stretching and snapping of rubber bands, and heavy sighing with no apparent cause for grief. Often F.P.S. goes unnoticed because the sufferer adopts the pose of staring off into the middle distance for indefinite lengths of time. Untrained observers are inclined to think he is absorbed in the awesome responsibility of high office. Hierarchiologists know otherwise.

Revealing Speech Habits

Baffling the Listener

Initial and Digital Codophilia is an obsession for speaking in letters and numbers rather than in words. For example, "F.O.B. is in N.Y. as O.C. for I.M.C. of B.U. on 802."

By the time, if ever, that the listener realizes that Frederick Orville Blamesworthy is in New York as Operative Co-ordinator for the Instructional Materials Center of Boondock University conducting business concerning Federal Bill 802, he has lost the opportunity to observe that the speaker did not really know much. Codophiliacs manage to make the trivial sound impressive, which is what they want.

Many Words, Few Thoughts

Some employees, on final placement, stop thinking, or at least sharply cut down on their thinking. To mask this, they develop lines of *General Purpose Conversation* or, in the case of public figures, *General Purpose Speeches*. These consist of remarks that sound impressive, yet which are vague enough to apply to all situations, with perhaps a few words changed each time to suit the particular audience.

My Executive Wastebasket and Trash Can Research Project * turned up the following notes, obviously fragments from the rough draft of an all-purpose speech. The writer has problems enough without my identifying him. My cause is education, not humiliation. Here are his notes:

Ladies and/or Gentlemen:
In these troublous times, it gives me great pleasure to speak to you on the important topic of ———. This is a subject in which fantastic advances have been made. We naturally —and rightly—take pride in our accomplishments locally, yet we must not omit a word of tribute to those individuals and groups who have made outstanding contributions on a larger scale, at the regional, national, yes, and—dare I say it?—the international level. . . .
While we must never underestimate the marvels that can be achieved by personal devotion, resolution and persistence, yet I suggest that it would be presumptuous for us to think that we can solve problems which have baffled the best brains of bygone and present generations. In conclusion, then, let me state my position without qualification or equivocation. I stand solidly behind progress; I call for

---

* This research method has been restricted. Some firms have installed locked trash cans in their offices to prevent piracy of ideas by competitors. A trash-disposal firm loads the trash cans' contents into a truck each day where at once all is turned into a grayish, unpiratable sand.

progress; I expect to see progress! Yet what I seek is true progress, not simply a chopping and changing for the mere sake of novelty. That true progress, friends, will be made, I suggest, only if, as and when we fix our minds, and keep them unshakably fixed, on our great historical heritage, and those magnificent traditions in which, now and forever, our real strength lies.

A Word to the Sufficient Is Wise

Look about you for the signs described above. They will greatly help you to analyze your fellow workers. But your most difficult task will be self-analysis. Hierarchiologist: heal thyself!

CHAPTER XIII

Health & Happiness at Zero PQ— Possibility or Pipe Dream?

"No sense have they of ills to come,
Nor care beyond today."

T. GRAY

———————

WHEN an employee reaches his Level of Incompetence (Peter's Plateau) he is said to have a Promotion Quotient (PQ) of zero.* In this chapter I shall show how different employees react to the situation.

Face the Sordid Truth (Not Recommended)

The employee realizes consciously that he has achieved final placement, reached his level of incompetence, bitten

———————

* The Promotion Quotient: a numerical expression of the employee's promotion prospects. When PQ declines to zero, he is completely in-

off more than he can chew, is out of his depth or "arrived." (These terms are synonymous.)

The type of employee who is capable of realizing this truth tends to equate incompetence with laziness; he assumes that he is not working hard enough, so he feels guilty.

He thinks that, by working harder, he will conquer the initial difficulties of the new position, and become competent. So he drives himself mercilessly, skips coffee breaks, works through his lunch hour and takes work home with him on evenings and weekends.

He rapidly falls victim to the Final Placement Syndrome.

Ignorance Is Bliss

Many an employee *never* realizes that he has reached his level of incompetence. He keeps perpetually busy, never loses his expectation of further promotion, and so remains *happy* and *healthy*.

You will naturally ask, "How does he do it?"

Substitution: The Lifesaver

Instead of carrying out the proper duties of his position he substitutes for them some other set of duties, which he carries out to perfection.

I will describe several Substitution techniques.

Technique No. 1: Perpetual Preparation

Faced with an important task, the competent employee simply begins it. The Substituter may prefer to busy him-

---

eligible for promotion. The PQ is fully explained in *The Peter Profile*, an unpublished monograph on the mathematical aspects of incompetence.

self with preliminary activities. Here are some well-tried methods.

a) CONFIRM THE NEED for action. The true Substituter can never get enough evidence. "Better be safe than sorry," is his watchword, or "More haste, less speed."

Spend sufficient time in confirming the need, and the need will disappear. (Peter's Prognosis.)

For example, in organizing famine relief, study the need long enough, and you will eventually find that there no longer is any need for relief!

b) STUDY ALTERNATE METHODS of doing whatever is to be done. Suppose that, after suitable preliminary investigation, the need is confirmed. The Substituter will want to be sure that he chooses the most efficient course of action, no matter how long he may take to find it. The "alternate method" technique is in itself a substitute and a less panicky form of the Teeter-Totter syndrome.

c) OBTAIN EXPERT ADVICE, in order that the plan finally chosen may be effectively carried out. Committees will be formed, and the question referred for study. A variant of this technique, looking to bygone experts instead of live ones, is to *search for precedents*.

d) FIRST THINGS FIRST. This technique involves minute, painstaking, time-consuming attention to every phase of preparation for action: the building-up of abundant reserves of spare forms, spare parts, spare ammunition, money, etc., in order to *consolidate the present position* before beginning an advance toward the goal.

Perpetual Preparation: An Instructive Example

Here is an interesting case which shows several of these techniques in use. Grant Swinger, deputy director of Deeprest Welfare Department, was regarded as highly competent because of his outstanding ability to coax governments and charitable foundations into parting with money for worthy local causes.

War was declared on poverty. Swinger was promoted to the post of co-ordinating director of the Deeprest Anti-Disadvantagement Program, on the principle that since he so well understood the mighty, he should be highly competent to help the weak.

As this goes to press, Swinger is still busily raising funds to erect an Olympian office building to house his staff and to stand as a permanent monument to the spirit of aiding the needy. (First Things First.)

"We want the poor to see that they have not been forgotten by their government," explains Swinger. Next he plans to convene a Deeprest Anti-Disadvantagement Advisory Council (obtaining expert advice), raise money for a survey of the problems of the disadvantaged (confirming the need) and tour the Western world to inspect similar schemes in preparation and operation elsewhere (studying alternate methods).

It should be pointed out that Swinger is busy from morning till night, is happy in his new post, and sincerely feels that he is doing a good job. He modestly turns away invitations to capitalize on his good image by running for elective office. In short he has achieved a highly successful *Substitution*.

Technique No. 2: Side-Issue Specialization

P. Gladman was promoted to manager of a rundown inefficient plant of the Sagamore Divan and Sofa Company, with the specific task of increasing production and making the branch pay.

He was incompetent for this task, realized it immediately and so quickly ceased to apply his mind to the question of productivity. He *Substituted* a zealous concern with the internal organization of the factory and office.

He spent his days assuring himself that there was no friction between management and labor, that working conditions were pleasant and that all employees of the branch were, as he put it, "one big, happy family."

Fortunately for Gladman he had taken with him, as assistant manager, D. Dominy, a young man who had not yet reached his level of incompetence. Thanks to Dominy's energetic action, the branch was revitalized and earned a handsome profit.

Gladman received the credit, and felt proud of his "success." He had appropriately *Substituted*, and achieved happiness in so doing.

The watchword for Side-Issue Specialists is *Look after the molehills and the mountains will look after themselves.*

U. Tredwell was a competent assistant principal in an Excelsior City elementary school, intellectually capable, maintaining good discipline among students and good morale among teachers. After promotion, he found his level of incompetence as principal: he lacked the tact necessary to deal with parents' organizations, newspaper reporters, the district superintendent of schools, and the elected members of the school board. He fell out of favor with the officials, and the reputation of his school began to decline in the eyes of the public.

Tredwell launched an ingenious Side-Issue Specialization. He developed an obsessive concern with the human traffic problems—with the swirls, eddies and bumps caused by movement of students and staff about halls, corridors, corners and stairways.

On large-scale plans of the building he worked out an elaborate system of traffic flow. He had lines and arrows painted in various colors on the walls and floors. He insisted on rigid observance of his traffic laws. No student was allowed to cross a white line. Suppose that one boy, during a lesson period, was sent from his classroom to take a message to a room immediately across the corridor. He could not cross the line down the middle: he had to walk right to the end of the corridor, go around the end of the line, then back down the other side of it.

Tredwell spent much time prowling the building looking for violations of his system; he wrote many articles about it for professional journals; he escorted visiting groups of Side-Issue-Specialist educators on tours of the building; he is at present engaged in writing a book on the subject, illustrated with many plans and photographs.

He is active and contented, and enjoys perfect health, with not the slightest sign of the Final Placement Syndrome. Another triumph for *Side-Issue Specialization!*

Technique No. 3: Image Replaces Performance

Mrs. Vender, an Excelsior City high-school mathematics teacher, spends a great deal of class time telling her pupils how interesting and important mathematics is. She lectures on the history, present state and probable future development of mathematics. The actual work of learning mathematics she assigns to the students as home study.

Mrs. Vender's classroom periods are bright and interesting; most of her pupils think she is a good teacher. They do not get on very well with the subject, but they believe that is just because it is so difficult.

Mrs. Vender, too, firmly believes that she is a good teacher; she thinks that only the jealousy of less competent teachers above her in the hierarchy bars her from promotion. So she enjoys a permanent, pleasant glow of self-righteousness.

Mrs. Vender is *Substituting*. Her technique is not uncommon, and it may be employed consciously or unconsciously. The rule is: for achieving personal satisfaction, *an ounce of image is worth a pound of performance*. (Peter's Placebo.)

Note that although this technique provides satisfaction to the user, it does not necessarily satisfy the employer!

Peter's Placebo is well understood by politicians at all levels. They will talk about the importance, the sacredness, the fascinating history of the democratic system (or the monarchic system, or the communist system or the tribal system as the case may be) but will do little or nothing toward carrying out the real duties of their position.

The technique is much used, too, in the arts. A. Fresco, a painter in Excelsior City, produced a few successful canvases and then appeared to run out of artistic inspiration. He then established his career as a speaker on the value of art. Typical is the *Saloon Writer* who sits in a bar all day, at home or overseas, talking about the importance of writing, the faults of other writers and the great works he himself is going to write some day.

Technique No. 4: Utter Irrelevance

This is a daring technique, and often succeeds for that very reason.

The *Perpetual Preparer,* the *Side-Issue Specialist* and the *Image Promoter,* as we have seen, are not accomplishing any useful work—at least, not what they should be doing— yet they are doing, or talking about, something that is in some way connected with the job. Sometimes casual observers—even colleagues—will not realize that these people are *Substituting* instead of producing results.

But the *Utter Irrelevantist* makes not the slightest pretense of doing his job.

F. Helps, president of Offset Wheel and Axle Inc., spends all his time serving on the directorates of charitable organizations: spearheading fund-raising campaigns, planning the philanthropic activity, heartening the volunteer workers and supervising the professionals. He comes to his own office only to sign a few important papers.

In his *Irrelevance,* Helps constantly rubs shoulders with a former antagonist—now a good friend—T. Merritt, life vice-president of the Wheel Truers' and Axle Keyers' Union. Merritt is on most of the same charitable committees as Helps and he, too, does nothing useful in his own office.

University boards of governors, government advisory panels and investigative commissions are happy hunting grounds for the *Utter Irrelevantists.*

In industrial and commercial hierarchies, this technique is usually seen at the upper levels only. However, in domestic hierarchies, it is exceedingly common at the housewives' level. Many a woman who has reached her level of

Leaving husband and children to look after themselves.

incompetence as wife and/or mother achieves a happy, successful *Substitution* by devoting her time and energy to *Utter Irrelevance* and leaving husband and children to look after themselves.

Technique No. 5: Ephemeral Administrology

Particularly in large, complex hierarchies, an incompetent senior employee can sometimes secure *temporary appointment* as acting director of another division, or pro tem chairman of some committee. The temporary work is substantially different from the employee's own regular job.

See how this works. The employee no longer has to cope with his own job (which he cannot do, anyway, having reached his level of incompetence), and he can justifiably refrain from taking any significant action in the new post.

"I can't make that decision: we must leave that for the permanent director, whenever he is appointed."

An adept *Ephemeral Administrator* may continue for years, filling one temporary post after another, and achieving sincere satisfaction from his *Substitution*.

Technique No. 6: Convergent Specialization

Finding himself incompetent to carry out all the duties of his position, the *Convergent Specialist* simply *ignores* most of them and concentrates his attention and efforts on one small task. If he is competent to do this, he will continue with it; if not, he will specialize still more narrowly.

F. Naylor, director of the Excelsior City Art Gallery, paid no attention to acquisition, exhibitions and financial policies, neglected building maintenance and spent all his time either working in the gallery's framing shop or researching for his *History of Picture Framing*. My latest information is that Naylor has realized that he will never learn all there is to know about framing; he has decided to concentrate on studying the *various types of glue* that have been used or may be used in picture framing.

A historian became the world's foremost authority on the first thirty minutes of the Reformation.

Several physicians have made reputations by studying some disease of which there are only three or four known cases, while others have become specialists who deal only in one small area of the body.

An academician who is incompetent to understand the meaning and value of a literary work may write a treatise titled, "A Comparative Study of the Use of the Comma in the Literary Works of Otto Scribbler."

Substitution Recommended

The examples I have cited, and others that doubtless occurred to you, show that, from the employee's point of view, *Substitution* is far and away the most satisfactory adjustment to final placement.

The achievement of an effective *Substitution* will usually prevent the development of the Final Placement Syndrome, and allow the employee to work out the rest of his career, healthy and self-satisfied, at his level of incompetence.

CHAPTER XIV

Creative Incompetence

"Always do one thing less than you think you can do."
B. M. BARUCH

D OES my exposition of the Peter Principle seem to you like a philosophy of despair? Do you shrink from the thought that final placement, with its wretched physical and psychological symptoms, must be the end of every career? Empathizing with these questions, I should like to present the reader with a knife that allows him to cut through this philosophical Gordian knot.

Better to Light a Single Candle than to Curse the Edison Co.

"Surely," you may say, "a person can simply refuse to accept promotion, and stay working happily at a job he can do competently."

An Interesting Example

The blunt refusal of an offered promotion is known as Peter's Parry. To be sure, it sounds easy enough. Yet I have discovered only one instance of its successful use.

T. Sawyer, a carpenter employed by the Beamish Construction Company, was so hard-working, competent and conscientious that he was several times offered the post of foreman.

Sawyer respected his boss and would have liked to oblige him. Yet he was happy as a rank-and-file carpenter. He had no worries: he could forget the job at 4:30 P.M. each day.

He knew that, as a foreman, he would spend his evenings and weekends worrying about the next day's and the next week's work. So he steadily refused the promotion.

Sawyer, it is worth noting, was an unmarried man with no close relatives and few friends. He could act as he pleased.

Not So Easy for Most of Us

For most people, Peter's Parry is impracticable. Consider the case of B. Loman, a typical citizen and family man, who refused a promotion.

His wife at once began to nag him. "Think of your children's future! What would the neighbours say if they knew? If you loved me, you'd want to get ahead!" and so on.

To find out for sure what the neighbours would say, Mrs. Loman confided the cause of her chagrin to a few trusted friends. The news spread around the district. Loman's young son, trying to defend his father's honor, fought one of his schoolmates and knocked out two of the other boy's teeth. The resulting litigation and dental bills cost Loman eleven hundred dollars.

Loman's mother-in-law worked Mrs. Loman's feelings up to such a pitch that she left him and secured a judicial separation. In his loneliness, disgrace and despair, he committed suicide.

No, refusing promotion is no easy route to happiness and health. I saw, early in my researches that, for most people, *Peter's Parry does not pay!*

An Illuminating Observation

While studying hierarchal structure and promotion rates among the production and clerical workers of the Ideal Trivet Company, I noticed that the grounds around the Trivet Building were beautifully landscaped and maintained. The velvety lawns and jewel-like flower beds suggested a high level of horticultural competence. I found that P. Greene, the gardener, was a happy, pleasant man with a genuine affection for his plants and a respect for his tools. He was doing what he liked best, gardening.

He was competent in all aspects of his work except one: he nearly always lost or mislaid receipts and delivery slips for goods received by his department, although he managed requisitions quite well.

The lack of delivery slips upset the accounting department, and Greene was several times reprimanded by the manager. His replies were vague.

"I think I may have planted the papers along with the shrubs."

"Maybe the mice in the potting shed got at the papers."

Because of this incompetence in paper work, when a new maintenance foreman was required, Greene was not considered for the post.

I interviewed Greene several times. He was courteous and

co-operative, but insisted that he lost the documents acci-
dentally. I questioned his wife. She told me that Greene
kept comprehensive records for his home gardening operations, and could calculate the cost of everything produced
in his yard or greenhouse.

A Parallel Case?

I interviewed A. Messer, shop foreman at Cracknell Cast-
ing and Foundry Company, whose little office seemed to
be in grotesque disorder. Nevertheless, my time-and-motion
study showed that the tottering piles of old account and
reference books, the cardboard cartons bursting with tat-
tered work sheets, the cabinets overflowing with unindexed
files and the sheaves of long-disused plans pinned to the
walls were really not a part of Messer's basically efficient
operation.

I could not tell whether he was or was not consciously
using this untidiness to camouflage his competence, in order
to avoid promotion to general foreman.

Madness in His Method?

J. Spellman was a competent schoolteacher. His professional reputation was high, yet he never got the offer of a
vice-principalship. I wondered why, and began to make in-
quiries.

A senior official told me, "Spellman neglects to cash his
pay checks. Every three months we have to remind him that
we would like him to cash his checks, so that we can keep
the books straight. I just can't understand a person who
doesn't cash his checks."

I questioned further.

"No, no! We don't distrust him," was the reply. "But

naturally one wonders whether he has some private source of income."

I asked, "Do you suspect that he might be involved in some illegal activities?"

"Certainly not! We don't have a shred of evidence against him. A fine teacher! A good man! A sterling reputation!"

Despite these disclaimers, I drew the inference that the hierarchy cannot trust a man who manages his finances so well that he does not rush to the bank and cash or deposit his pay check in order to cover his bills. Spellman, in short, had shown himself incompetent to behave as the typical employee is expected to behave; hence he had made himself ineligible for promotion.

Was it *only* coincidence that Spellman was happy in his teaching work, and had no desire for promotion to administrative duties?

Was it only coincidence that Spellman was happy in his teaching work?

Is There a Pattern?

I investigated many similar cases of what seemed to be deliberate incompetence, but I could never certainly decide whether the behavior was the result of conscious planning, or of a subconscious motivation.

One thing was clear: these employees had avoided advancement, not by refusing promotion—we have already seen how disastrous that can be—but by contriving never to be offered a promotion!

Eureka!

This is an infallible way to *avoid the ultimate promotion;* this is *the key to health and happiness* at work and in private life; this is *Creative Incompetence.*

A Proven Policy

It does not matter whether Greene, Messer, Spellman and other employees similarly situated are consciously or unconsciously avoiding the ultimate promotion. What does matter is that we can learn from them how to achieve this vitally important goal. ("Vitally important" is no figure of speech: the correct technique may save your life.)

The method boils down to this: *create the impression that you have already reached your level of incompetence.*

You do this by exhibiting one or more of the non-medical symptoms of final placement.

Greene the gardener was exhibiting a mild form of Papyrophobia. Messer, the foundry foreman, to a casual observer, seemed to be an Advanced Papyromaniac. Spellman the schoolteacher, procrastinating over the deposit of his pay checks, showed a severe, though unusual, form of the Teeter-Totter Syndrome.

Creative Incompetence will achieve best results if you choose an area of incompetence *which does not directly hinder you in carrying out the main duties of your present position.*

Some Subtle Techniques

For a clerical worker, such an unspectacular habit as leaving one's desk drawers open at the end of the working day will, in some hierarchies, have the desired effect.

A show of niggling, officious economy—the switching off of lights, turning off of taps, picking up paper clips and rubber bands off the floor and out of wastebaskets, to the accompaniment of muttered homilies on the value of thrift —is another effective maneuver.

Stand Out from the Crowd

Refusal to pay one's share of the firm's or department's Social Fund; refraining from drinking coffee at the official coffee break; bringing one's own lunch to a job where everyone else eats out; persistent turning off of radiators and opening of windows; refusing contributions to collections for wedding and retirement gifts; a mosaic of stand-offish eccentricity (the Diogenes Complex) will create just the modicum of suspicion and distrust which disqualifies you for promotion.

AUTOMOTIVE TACTICS   One highly successful department manager avoided promotion by occasionally parking his car in the space reserved for the company president.

Another executive always drove a car one year older, and five hundred dollars cheaper in original price, than the cars of his peers.

PERSONAL APPEARANCE　Most people agree *in principle* with the dictum that fine feathers don't make fine birds, but *in practice* an employee is judged by his appearance. Here, then, is ample scope for Creative Incompetence.

The wearing of unconventional or *slightly* shabby clothes, irregularity of bathing, *occasional* neglect of haircutting or *occasional* carelessness in shaving (the *small* but conspicuous wound dressing adjoining a *small* blob of congealed blood, or the small patch of stubble missed by the razor) are useful techniques.

Ladies may wear *a shade too much* or *too little* makeup, possibly combined with the *occasional* wearing of an unbecoming or inappropriate hair style. Overly strong perfume and overly brilliant jewelry work well in many cases.

MORE REAL-LIFE EXAMPLES　Here, for your guidance and inspiration, are some superb instances of Creative Incompetence which I have observed * in my studies.

Mr. F. proposed to the boss's daughter at the firm's annual Founder's Birthday Party. The girl had just graduated from a European finishing school, and F. had never seen her before that occasion. Naturally, he did not get the daughter and naturally, too, he rendered himself ineligible for promotion.

---

* At least I *think* I have observed them. The mark of *perfect* Creative Incompetence is that no one, *even the trained hierarchiologist,* can ever be *sure* it is not just plain incompetence.

Mr. F. proposed to the boss's daughter.

Miss L. of the same firm, contrived to offend the boss's wife at the same party by imitating the older woman's peculiar laugh within her hearing.

Mr. P. got a friend to make *one* fake threatening phone call to him at the office. Within earshot and sight of his colleagues P. reacted dramatically, begged for "mercy" and "more time" and pleaded, "Don't tell my wife. If she finds out this will kill her." Was this just one of P.'s typically stupid jokes, or was it an inspired piece of Creative Incompetence?

An Old Friend Revisited

I recently reviewed the case of T. Sawyer, the carpenter whose successful use of Peter's Parry I described at the beginning of this chapter.

In the last few months he has been buying cheap paperbound copies of *Walden* * and giving them away to his workmates and superiors, in each case with a few remarks on the pleasures of irresponsibility and the joys of day labor.

He follows up the gift with persistent questioning to see whether the recipient has read the book and how much of it he has understood. This meddlesome didacticism I denominate *The Socrates Complex.*

Sawyer reports that the offers of promotion have ceased. I naturally felt a little disappointment at the disappearance of the only living example of a *successful* Peter's Parry (successful in the sense that it had averted proffered promotion without causing him unhappiness). Yet this disappointment was counterbalanced by pleasure at seeing an elegant proof of the fact that

Creative Incompetence Beats Peter's Parry— Every Time!

An Important Precaution

A thoughtful study of Chapter 12 will give you plenty of ideas for developing your own form of Creative Incompetence. Yet I must emphasize the paramount importance of *concealing the fact that you want to avoid promotion!*

---

* Thoreau, Henry D. (1817–62). *Walden, or Life in the Woods,* 1854.

As camouflage, you may even indulge in the occasional mild *grumble* to your peers: "Darned funny how *some* people get promotion in this place, while others are passed over!"

Dare You Do It?

If you have not yet attained final placement on Peter's Plateau, you can discover an irrelevant incompetence.

Find it and practice it diligently. It will keep you at a level of competence and so assure you of the keen personal satisfaction of regularly accomplishing some useful work.

Surely creative incompetence offers as great a challenge as the traditional drive for higher rank!

CHAPTER XV

The Darwinian Extension

"The meek . . . shall inherit the earth."
JESUS OF NAZARETH

I N discussing competence and incompetence we have so far dealt mainly with vocational problems—with the toils and stratagems men use to make a living in a complex, industrialized society.

This chapter will apply the Peter Principle to a broader issue, to the question of *life-competence*. Can the human race hold its position, or advance, in the evolutionary hierarchy?

The Peterian Interpretation of History

Man has achieved many promotions in the life-hierarchy. Each promotion thus far—from tree dweller to caveman, to fire lighter, to flint knapper, to stone polisher, to bronze smelter, to iron founder and so on—has increased his prospects of survival as a species.

The more conceited members of the race think in terms of an endless ascent—or promotion *ad infinitum.* I would point out that, sooner or later, *man must reach his level of life-incompetence.*

Two things could prevent this happening: that there should not be enough time available, or not enough ranks in the hierarchy. But, so far as we can ascertain, there is infinite time ahead of us (whether we are here to take advantage of it or not), and there are an infinite number of ranks in existence or in potential (various religions have described whole hierarchies of angels, demigods and gods above the present level of humanity).

Other species have achieved many promotions, only to reach their levels of life-incompetence. The dinosaur, the saber-toothed tiger, the pterodactyl, the mammoth developed and flourished by virtue of certain qualities—bulk, fangs, wings, tusks. But the very qualities which at first assured their promotion eventually brought about their incompetence. We might say that *competence always contains the seed of incompetence.* General Goodwin's vulgar bonhomie, Miss Ditto's unoriginality, Mr. Driver's dominant personality—*these were the qualities which gained them promotion; these same qualities eventually barred them from further promotion!* So various animal species, after eons of steady promotion, have reached the levels of incompetence and have become static, or have achieved superincompetence and have become extinct.

This has happened to many human societies and civilizations. Some people who flourished in colonial status, under the tutelage of stronger nations, have proved incompetent when promoted to self-government. Other nations that competently ruled themselves as city-states, republics or monarchies, have proved incompetent to survive as imperial powers. Civilizations that thrived on adversity and hardship proved incompetent to stand the strains of success and affluence.

What of the human race as a whole? *Cleverness* is the quality which has won for mankind promotion after promotion. Will that cleverness prove a bar to further promotion? Will it even reduce mankind to the condition of super-incompetence (see Chapter 3) and thus ensure his speedy dismissal from the life-hierarchy?

Two Ominous Signs

1. Hierarchal Regression

It is through the schools that society begins its task of molding and training the new members of the human race. I have already examined a typical school system as it concerns the teachers who staff it. Now let us look at school as it affects the pupils.

The old-fashioned school system was a pure expression of the Peter Principle. A pupil was promoted, grade by grade, until he reached his level of incompetence. Then he was said to have "failed" Grade 5 or 8 or 11, etc. He would have to "repeat the grade"; that is, he would have to remain at his level of incompetence. In some instances, because the child was still growing mentally, his intellectual competence would increase during the "repeating" year, and he would then become eligible for further promotion. If not, he would "fail" again, and "repeat" again.

(It is worth noting that this "failure" is the same thing

that, in vocational studies, we call "success," namely, the attainment of final placement at the level of incompetence.)

School officials do not like this system: they think that the accumulation of incompetent students lowers the standard within the school. One administrator told me, "I wish I could pass all the dull pupils and fail the bright ones: that would raise standards and grades would improve. This hoarding of dull students lowers the standard by reducing the average achievement in my school."

Such an extreme policy will not be generally tolerated. So, to avoid the accumulation of incompetents, administrators have evolved the plan of promoting everyone, *the incompetent as well as the competent*. They find psychological justification for this policy by saying that it spares students the painful experience of failure.

What they are actually doing is *applying percussive sublimation* to the incompetent students.

The result of this wholesale percussive sublimation is that high-school graduation may now represent the same level of scholastic achievement as did Grade 11 a few years ago. In time, graduation will sink in value to the level of the old Grade 10, Grade 9 and so on.

This phenomenon I designate *hierarchal regression*.

Results of Hierarchal Regression

Educational certificates, diplomas and degrees are losing their value as measures of competence. Under the old system we knew that a pupil who "failed" Grade 8 must at least have been competent in Grade 7. We knew that a pupil who "failed" first-year university must at least have been a competent high-school graduate, and so on.

But now we cannot assume any such thing. The modern certificate proves only that the pupil *was competent to endure a certain number of years' schooling*.

High-school graduation, once a widely accepted certificate of competence, is now only a certificate of incompetence for most responsible, well-paid jobs.*

So it goes at the post-high-school level. Bachelors' and masters' degrees have regressed in value. Only the doctorate still carries any notable aura of competence, and its value is rapidly being eroded by the emergence of post-doctoral degrees. How long will it be before the post-doctorate, too, becomes a badge of incompetence for many posts, and the earnest striver will have to plow on through post-post and post-post-post doctorates?

Escalation of educational effort speeds the process of degradation. Many universities, for example, now use the very same pupil-teacher system (older students teaching younger students) which fifty years ago was being condemned in the grade schools!

Escalation of effort in any other field produces comparable results. Under the pressure to get *more* engineers, scientists, priests, teachers, automobiles, apples, spacemen or what have you, and to get them faster, the standards of acceptance necessarily sink: hierarchal regression sets in.

You, as a consumer, an employer, an artisan or teacher, no doubt see the results of hierarchal regression. I shall re-

---

* It is noteworthy that hierarchal regression is not entirely a modern phenomenon. Many years ago, literacy was itself regarded as a certificate of competence for most important positions. Then it was found that there was an increasing number of literate fools, so employers began to raise their standards—fifth grade, eighth grade, and so on. Each of these standards began as a certificate of competence; each was finally regarded as a certificate of incompetence.

turn to the subject later, to suggest ways in which it might be controlled.

2. Computerized Incompetence

A drunken man is temporarily incompetent to steer a straight course. So long as he is on foot, he is a danger chiefly to himself. But put him at the wheel of an automobile and he may kill a score of other people before he breaks his own neck.

The point needs no laboring. Obviously, the more powerful the means at my disposal, the greater good or harm I can do by my competence or incompetence.

The printing press, radio, television have in turn expanded man's power to propagate and perpetuate his incompetence. Now comes the computer.

Computer Use File: Case No. 11

R. Fogg, founder and managing director of Fogg Interlocking Blocks, Inc., was an inventor-engineer who had reached his level of incompetence as an administrator. Fogg constantly complained about the poor performance of his office manager, clerks and accountants. He did not realize that they were about as efficient as most similar groups of employees. Some of them were not yet at their levels of incompetence; they turned out some work and kept the business going. They managed to take Fogg's muddled instructions, separate what had best be ignored from what would be of some use to the company, and then took appropriate action.

A salesman convinced Fogg that a computer could be programmed to do much of the work of his office staff as well as improve efficiency of the plant. Fogg placed the order, the computer was installed, and the "surplus" staff was dismissed.

But Fogg soon found that the work of the firm was not being handled so fast or so well as before. There were two points about a computer that he had not understood. (At least, he had not understood that they would apply to his operations.)

a) A computer balks at any unclear instruction, simply blinks its lights and waits for clarification.

b) A computer has no tact. It will not flatter. It will not use judgment. It will not say, "Yes, sir; at once, sir!" to wrong instructions, then go away and do the job right. It will simply follow the wrong orders, so long as they are clearly given.

Fogg's business ran rapidly downhill and within a year his company was bankrupt. He had fallen victim to *Computerized Incompetence*.

MORE HORRIBLE EXAMPLES. The Quebec Department of Education wrongly paid out $275,864 in student loans. The mistake was made by computer-directed multi-copying services.

In New York a bank computer went on the blink; three billion dollars' worth of accounts went unbalanced for twenty-four hours.

The computer belonging to an airline printed 6,000 instead of ten replenishment notices. The airline found itself with 5,990 surplus orders of mint chocolates.

A study made in 1966 shows that over 70 percent of computer installations made to that time in Britain must be considered commercially unsuccessful.

One computer was so sensitive to static electricity that

it made errors every time it was approached by a female employee wearing nylon lingerie.

Three Observations

1) The computer may be incompetent in itself—that is, unable to do regularly and accurately the work for which it was designed. This kind of incompetence can never be eliminated, because the Peter Principle applies in the plants where computers are designed and manufactured.

2) Even when competent in itself, the computer vastly magnifies the results of incompetence in its owners or operators.

3) The computer, like a human employee, is subject to the Peter Principle. If it does good work at first, there is a strong tendency to promote it to more responsible tasks, until it reaches its level of incompetence.

The Signs Interpreted

These two signs—the rapid spread of hierarchal regression and computerized incompetence—are only part of a general trend which, if continued, will escalate inevitably to the Total-Life-Incompetence level. In Chapter 3 you saw that the obsessive concern for *input* could eventually destroy the purpose for which the hierarchy existed (*output*). Here we see that the thoughtless escalation of educational effort and the automation of outmoded or incorrect methods are examples of this mindless kind of input. Our leaders in politics, science, education, industry and the military have insisted that we go as fast as we can and as far as we can inspired only by blind faith that *great input* will produce *great output*.

As a student of hierarchiology you now realize that society's continued escalation of input is simply *Peter's Inversion* on a grand scale.

Man's First Mistake: The Wheel

Look at the results. Conceivably we are all doomed by our own cleverness and devotion to escalation. Our land, a few decades ago, was dotted with crystal-clear lakes and laced with streams of cool, clear water. The soil produced wholesome food. Citizens had easy access to rural scenes of calm beauty.

Now lakes and streams are cesspools. Air is noxious with smoke, soot and smog. Land and water are poisoned with pesticides, so that birds, bees, fish, and cattle are dying. The countryside is a dump for garbage and old automobiles.

This is progress! We have made so much progress that we cannot even speak with confidence about the prospect of

Citizens had easy access to rural scenes of calm beauty.

human survival. We have blighted the promise of this century and converted the miracles of science into a chamber of horrors where a nuclear holocaust could become a death-trap for the entire human race. If we continue feverishly planning and inventing and building and rebuilding for more of this progress, we will achieve the level of *Total-Life-Incompetence*.

New Social Science Shows the Way

Do you sometimes feel you have a rendezvous with oblivion but would prefer to break the date? Hierarchiology can show you how.

Of all proposals for betterment of the human condition and survival of the human race only one, the Peter Principle, realistically embodies factual knowledge about the human organism. Hierarchiology reveals man's true nature, his perpetual production of hierarchies, his quest for means of maintaining them, and his countervailing tendency to destroy them. The Peter Principle and hierarchiology provide the unifying factor for all social sciences.

Peter's Remedies

Must the whole human race achieve life-incompetence and earn dismissal from the life-hierarchy?

Before you answer this question, ask yourself, "What is the purpose (output) of the human hierarchy?"

In my lecture, *Destiny Lies Ahead,* I tell my students, "If you don't know where you are going, you will probably end up somewhere else."

Obviously, if the purpose of the hierarchy is total human

exfoliation, Peter's Remedies are not needed. But if we wish to survive, and to better our condition, Peter's Remedies, ranging from prevention to cure, will show the way.

I offer:

1. Peter's Prophylactics—means to avoid promotion to the level of incompetence.

2. Peter's Palliatives—for those who have already reached their level of incompetence, means for prolonging life and maintaining health and happiness.

3. Peter's Placebos—for suppression of the symptoms of the Final Placement Syndrome.

4. Peter's Prescriptions—cures for the world's ills.

1. Peter's Prophylactics—An Ounce of Prevention

A prophylactic, in the hierarchiological sense, is a preventive measure applied before the Final Placement Syndrome appears, or before Hierarchal Regression sets in.

The Power of Negative Thinking

I strongly recommend the health-giving power of negative thinking. If Mr. Mal d'Mahr had thought about the negative aspects of the chief executive's post, would he have accepted the promotion?

Suppose he had asked, "What will the directors think of me? What will my subordinates expect? What will my wife expect?"

If Mal had dwelt steadily on the negative aspects of promotion, would he have halted the course of action that destroyed his health?

He was intellectually competent; he could have added up the negatives, including the conflict of codes described earlier, the changed relationships with his friends, the pressure to join the country club, the need to own a dress suit, his wife's demands for a new wardrobe, the community's request that he head fund-raising drives, and all the other pressures associated with the promotion.

He might well have decided that life at his old level was actually fulfillment, that he was satisfied where he was, and that his status, social life, avocations and *health* were worth protecting.

You can apply the power of negative thinking. Ask yourself, "How would I like to work for my boss's boss?"

Look, not at your boss, whom you think you could replace, but at *his* boss. How would you like to work directly for the man two steps above you? The answer to this question often has prophylactic benefits.

In dealing with incompetence on the civic, national or world-wide scale, the power of negative thinking has great potential.

Consider the merits of a costly undersea exploration program, for example. Contemplate the discomforts and hazards of life on the sea bed; contrast them with the comfort and safety of an afternoon beside the swimming pool or an evening party at the beach.

Consider the stench, bad flavors and perils involved in spraying the entire globe with pesticides: compare them with the simple pleasure, and the therapeutic exercise, of hand-spraying the garden.

The power of negative thinking can help us avoid escalating ourselves to a level of life-incompetence, and so help prevent destruction of the world.

Another Prophylactic—Creative Incompetence

As another approach to the great problem of man's life-incompetence, let us consider application of creative incompetence. We need not give up the *appearance* of striving for promotion in the life-hierarchy, but we could deliberately practice *irrelevant incompetence* so as to bar ourselves from obtaining that promotion.

(By "irrelevant" I mean "not connected with getting food, keeping warm, maintaining a healthful environment, and raising children, the essential elements for survival.")

Here is an example. Man has competently solved many problems of transport on and about the world he inhabits. At no great expenditure of time, he can travel to any part of the globe, with no more hardship or danger than he endures in walking the streets of his own town. (With considerably *less* danger, if he happens to live in a major city!)

Promotion in the travel-hierarchy would be expected to advance man from earth traveller to space traveller. But this would be escalation for its own sake. Man has no need to explore the moon, Mars or Venus in person. He has already sent radar, TV and photographic instruments which transmit vivid descriptions of these heavenly bodies. The reports suggest that they are inhospitable places.

Man would be better off without the promotion to space traveller. But, as we have seen, it is no easy thing to *refuse* a promotion. The safe, pleasant, effective way is to seem *not to deserve it:* this is creative incompetence.

Man now has the chance to exhibit creative incompetence in this field of space travel.* He has the chance to curb his

---

* The bungles, delays and disaster associated with space travel indicate that the people concerned with it *may,* indeed, be exercising creative

dangerous cleverness and show a little wholesome incompetence.

THE MALADY LINGERS ON   Let us look at another example. Man has moved up the therapeutic hierarchy, through magic, voodoo, faith healing, to modern, orthodox medicine and surgery. He is now very near to fabricating human beings out of spare parts, natural and synthetic. This step would promote him from healer to creator.

But, faced with a population explosion and with widespread starvation, what need has man to accept that promotion?

Would it not be timely to exhibit creative incompetence at this point, to bungle the creative technique, and so avoid the useless, the potentially dangerous, promotion?

It's Up to You

By a little thought, you will be able to find other areas in which this creative incompetence—this meekness—might well be applied.

Faced with the possibility of promotion to the level of Total-Life-Incompetence—say through atmospheric pollution, nuclear war, global starvation or invasion of Martian bacteria—we would be well advised to use Peter's Prophylactics.

If we practice negative thinking and creative incompetence, and thereby avoid taking the final step, the possibility of human survival would be enhanced. *Peter's Prophylactics prevent pathological promotions.*

---

incompetence. I emphasize "may" because the test of real creative incompetence is that an observer cannot certainly tell whether the incompetence is deliberate or not.

2. Peter's Palliatives—An Ounce of Relief

Although the human race, as a whole, has not yet reached its level of Total-Life-Incompetence, many individuals, as we saw earlier, do reach that level, and fairly rapidly remove themselves from this world.

I have already discussed some palliatives for these people—measures that can enable them to live out their lives in comparative happiness and comfort. Now let us see how such palliatives can be applied on a larger scale.

Hierarchal Regression Stopped!

As we saw earlier, hierarchal regression in an educational system is caused by mass percussive sublimation of pupils who, in olden days, would have been allowed to "fail."

I propose, instead of using percussive sublimation, to give such students the *lateral arabesque*.

At present, a student who "fails" Grade 8 is sublimated to Grade 9. Under my plan, he would be arabesqued from Grade 8 to a year, say, of Freshman Academic Depth Study. He could then repeat his year's work, preferably with special emphasis on the points that he failed to understand before. The extra experience, his own growing maturity and—with luck—more competent teaching, might prepare him for Grade 9.

If not, his parents could hardly object to his "winning" a two-year Fellowship in Higher Academic Depth Study.

Eventually, if the pupil made no further progress by school-leaving age, he would be awarded a certificate making him a Life Fellow of Academic Depth Study.

Thus the lateral arabesque lets him out sideways. It does not interfere with the education of the pupils who are still moving upward, and it does not diminish the worth of the grades and degrees which those upward-moving pupils achieve.

The technique has proved successful with individuals at work. Why not try it on a big scale in the educational field? *Peter's Palliative prevents percussive sublimation.*

3. Peter's Placebo—An Ounce of Image

Hierarchiologically speaking, a Placebo is the application of a neutral (non-escalatory) methodology to suppress the undesirable results of reaching a level of incompetence.

I would like to refer again to the case of Mrs. Vender, cited in Chapter 13. Mrs. Vender, at her level of incompetence, did not spend her time teaching mathematics, but in extolling the value of mathematics.

Mrs. Vender was *substituting image for performance.* Peter's Placebo: an ounce of image is worth a pound of performance.

Now let us see how the Placebo can be applied on the grand scale. Incompetent workers, instead of striving for promotion, would lecture eloquently on *the dignity of labor.* Incompetent educators would give up teaching and spend their time extolling *the value of education.* Incompetent painters would promote *the appreciation of art.* Incompetent space travellers would *write science fiction.* Sexually incompetent persons would *compose love lyrics.*

All such practitioners of Peter's Placebo might not be doing much good, but at least, *they would be doing no harm,* and they would not be interfering with the operations of competent members of the various trades and professions. *Peter's Placebo prevents professional paralysis.*

4. Peter's Prescription—A Pound of Cure

What might be the results, for the human race, of applying Peter's Prescription?

Peter's Prophylactics would prevent millions of people from ever reaching their levels of incompetence. Consequently those same millions who, under the present system, are frustrated and unproductive, would remain, all their lives, happy and useful members of society.

Peter's Palliatives and Placebos would ensure that those who had achieved their levels of incompetence were kept harmlessly busy, happy and healthy. This change would set free for productive work the millions of people presently employed in looking after the health, and repairing the blunders, of all those incompetents.

The net result? An enormous store of man-hours, of creativity, of enthusiasm, would be set free for constructive purposes.

We might, for instance, develop safe, comfortable, efficient rapid-transit systems for our major cities. (They would cost less than moonships and serve more people.)

We might tap power sources (*e.g.,* generator plants powered by smokeless trash burners) which would not pollute the atmosphere. Thus we would contribute to the better health of our people, the beautification of our scenery and the better visibility of that more beautiful scenery.

We might improve the quality and safety of our automobiles, landscape our freeways, highways and avenues, and so restore some measure of safety and pleasure to surface travel.

We might learn to return to our farm lands organic products that would enrich, without poisoning, the soil.

Much waste that is now dumped might be salvaged and converted into new products, using collection systems as complex as our present distribution systems.

Otherwise useless waste might be dumped to fill abandoned open-pit mines and reclaim the land for constructive purposes.

You Figure It Out

Space permits no further elaboration. You, as a serious reader, will be able to see the application of Peter's Prescription * in your life and work, and in the life and work of your city, country and planet.

You will agree that man cannot achieve his greatest fulfillment through seeking quantity for quantity's sake: he will achieve it through improving the *quality of life,* in other words, through avoiding life-incompetence.

Peter's Prescription offers life-quality-improvement in place of mindless promotion to oblivion.

Hierarchiology in the Ascendant

I have said enough to indicate that your happiness, health and joy of accomplishment, as well as the hope for man's future, lies in understanding the Peter Principle, in applying the principles of hierarchiology, and in utilizing Peter's Prescription to solve human problems.

I have written this book so that you can understand and use the Peter Principle. Its acceptance and application is up to you. Other books will doubtless follow. In the meantime,

---

* I have applied this to education. (See *Prescriptive Teaching,* by Laurence J. Peter, New York: McGraw-Hill Book Co., 1965.)

Man will achieve his greatest fulfillment through improving the quality of life.

let us hope that a philanthropist somewhere will soon endow a chair of hierarchiology at a major university. When he does I am qualified and ready for the post, having proven myself capable in my present endeavours.

Glossary

Alger Complex—a moralistic delusion concerning the effect of Push on promotion. Chap. 5.

Alternation, compulsive—a technique for flustering subordinates. Chap. 12.

Aptitude tests—a popular means of hastening final placement. Chap. 9.

Arrived—achieved final placement. Chap. 3.

Auld Lang Syne Complex—sentimental belittlement of things present and glorification of things past: a sign of final placement. Chap. 12.

Buckpass, Downward, Upward and Outward—techniques for avoiding responsibility. Chap. 12.

Cachinatory Inertia—telling jokes instead of working. Chap. 12.

Caesarian Transference—irrational prejudice against some physical characteristic. Chap. 12.

Codophilia, Initial and Digital—speaking in letters and numbers instead of words. Chap. 12.

Comparative Hierarchiology—an incomplete study. Chap. 7.

Competence—the employee's ability, as measured by his superiors, to fill his place in the hierarchy. Chap. 3.

Compulsive Incompetence—a condition exhibited by Summit Competents. (See "Summit Competence.")

Computerized Incompetence—incompetent application of computer techniques or the inherent incompetence of a computer. Chap. 15.

Convergent Specialization—a Substitution technique. Chap. 13.

Cooks—makers of broth, some incompetent. Chap. 8.

Co-ordinator—an employee charged with the task of extracting competence from incompetents. Chap. 9.

Copelessness—a condition occasionally understood by employees, more often by management. Chap. 9.

Creative Incompetence—feigned incompetence which averts the offer of unwanted promotion. Chap. 14.

Deadwood—an accumulation at any level in a hierarchy of employees who have reached their level of incompetence.

Distraction Therapy—a treatment for relief of the Final Placement Syndrome. Chap. 11.

Edifice Complex—a complex about buildings. Chap. 12.

Einstein, Albert—mathematician and trend setter in men's fashions. Chap. 9.

Eligible—any employee who competently carries out his duties is eligible for promotion.

Emotion-laden terms—not used in hierarchiology. Chap. 9.

Ephemeral Administrology—a Substitution technique. Chap. 9.

Equalitarianism—a social system which ensures the freest and fastest operation of the Peter Principle. Chap. 7.

Exceptions—there are no exceptions to the Peter Principle.

Failure (as applied to school pupils)—see "Success."

Fileophilia—a mania for classification of papers. Chap. 12.

Final Placement Syndrome—pathology associated with placement at the level of incompetence. Chap. 11.

First Commandment—"The hierarchy must be preserved." Chap. 3.

First things first—a Substitution technique. Chap. 13.

Free-Floating Apex—a supervisor with no subordinates. Chap. 3.

Funds—needed by Professor Peter. Chap. 7.

Gargantuan Monumentalis—giant burial park, big mausoleum and huge tombstone syndrome. Chap. 12.

General Purpose Conversation—stock, meaningless phrases. Chap. 12.

Good follower—supposedly a good leader: a fallacy. Chap. 6.

Heep Syndrome—a group of symptoms indicating the patient's belief in his own worthlessness. Observed by D. Copperfield, reported by C. Dickens. Chap. 9.

Hierarchal Exfoliation—the sloughing-off of super-competent and super-incompetent employees. Chap. 3.

Hierarchal Regression—result of promoting the incompetent along with the competent. Chap. 15.

Hierarchiology—a social science, the study of hierarchies, their structure and functioning, the foundation for all social science.

Hierarchy—an organization whose members or employees are arranged in order of rank, grade or class.

Hierarchy, Cheopsian or feudal—a pyramidal structure with many low-ranking and few high-ranking employees. Chap. 8.

Hull's Theorem—"The combined Pull of several Patrons is the sum of their separate Pulls multiplied by the number of Patrons." Chap. 4.

Hypercaninophobia Complex—fear caused in superiors when an inferior demonstrates strong leadership potential. Chap. 6.

Image Replaces Performance—a Substitution technique. Chap. 13.

Incompetence—a null quantity: incompetence plus incompetence equals incompetence. Chap. 10.

Input—activities which support the rules, rituals and forms of a hierarchy. Chap. 3.

John Q. Diversion—undue reliance on public opinion. Chap. 12.

Lateral Arabesque—a pseudo-promotion consisting of a new title and a new work place. Chap. 3.

Leadership competence—disqualification for promotion. Chap. 6.

Level of Competence—a position in a hierarchy at which an employee more or less does what is expected of him.

Level of Incompetence—a position in a hierarchy at which an employee is unable to do what is expected of him.

Life-Incompetence Syndrome—a cause of frustration. Chap. 8.

Maturity Quotient—a measure of the inefficiency of a hierarchy. Chap. 7.

Medical Profession—a group showing apathy and hostility toward hierarchiology. Chap. 11.

Meekness—a technique of Creative Incompetence. Chap. 15.

Obtain expert advice—a Substitution technique. Chap. 13.

Order—"Heav'n's first law": the basis of the hierarchal instinct. Chap. 8.

Output—the performance of useful work. Chap. 3.

Papyromania—compulsive accumulation of papers. Chap. 12.

Papyrophobia—abnormal desire for "a clean desk." Chap. 12.

Party—a hierarchal organization for selecting candidates for political office. Chap. 7.

Patron—one who speeds the promotion of employees lower in the hierarchy. Chap. 4.

Percussive Sublimation—being kicked upstairs: a pseudo-promotion. Chap. 3.

Peter Principle—In a hierarchy, every employee tends to rise to his level of incompetence.

Peter's Bridge—an important test: can you motivate your Patron? Chap. 4.

Peter's Circumambulation—a circumlocution or detour around a super-incumbent. Chap. 4.

Peter's Circumbendibus—a veiled or secretive circumambulation (see above).

Peter's Corollary—In time, every post in a hierarchy tends to be occupied by an employee who is incompetent to carry out its duties.

Peter's Inversion—internal consistency valued more highly than efficiency. Chap. 3.

Peter's Invert—one for whom means have become ends in themselves. Chap. 3.

Peter's Nuance—the difference between Pseudo-Achievement and Final Placement Syndromes. Chap. 5.

Peter's Palliatives—provide relief for incompetence symptoms. Chap. 15.

Peter's Paradox—employees in a hierarchy do not really object to incompetence in their colleagues. Chap. 4.

Peter's Parry—the refusal of an offered promotion. (Not recommended.) Chap. 14.

Peter's Placebo—An ounce of image is worth a pound of performance. Chap. 13.

Peter's Plateau—the level of incompetence.

Peter's Prescriptions—CURES for individual or world ills. Chap. 15.

Peter's Pretty Pass—the situation of having one's road to promotion blocked by a super-incumbent. Chap. 4.

Peter's Prognosis—Spend sufficient time in confirming the need, and the need will disappear. Chap. 13.

Peter's Prophylactics—an ounce of prevention. Chap. 15.

Peter's Remedies—means of preventing total-life-incompetence. Chap. 15.

Peter's Spiral—the non-progressive course followed by organizations suffering from high-level incompetence. Chap. 10.

Peterian Interpretation—the application of hierarchiological science to the facts and fictions of history. Chap. 15.

Phonophilia—an abnormal desire for possession and use of voice transmission and recording equipment. Chap. 12.

Professional Automatism—an obsessive concern with rituals and a disregard of results. Chap. 3.

Promotion—an upward movement from a level of competence.

Promotion Quotient—numerical expression of promotion prospects. Chap. 13.

Protégé—see "Pullee."

Proto-hierarchiologists—authors who might have contributed to hierarchiological thought. Chap. 8.

Proverbs—as repositories of hierarchiological fallacies. Chap. 8.

Pseudo-Achievement Syndrome—a complex of physical ailments resulting from excessive Push. Chap. 5.

Pull—an employee's relationship—by blood, marriage or acquaintance—with a person above him. Chap. 4.

Pullee—an employee who has Pull. Chap. 4.

Random Placement—a cause of delay in reaching the level of incompetence. Chap. 9.

Rigor Cartis—abnormal interest in charts, with dwindling concern for realities that the charts represent. Chap. 12.

Saints—good men but incompetent controversialists. Chap. 8.

Secrecy—the soul of Push. Chap. 5.

Seniority Factor—downward pressure which opposes the upward movement of competent employees. Chap. 5.

Side-Issue Specialization—a Substitution technique. Chap. 13.

Socrates Complex—a form of Creative Incompetence. Chap. 14.

Staticmanship—the timely renunciation of One-upmanship. Chap. 8.

Study alternate methods—a Substitution technique. Chap. 13.

Substitution—a lifesaving technique for employees on Peter's Plateau. Chap. 13.

Success—final placement at the level of incompetence. Chap. 8.

Summit Competence—a rare condition. Chap. 9.

Super-competence—doing one's work too well: a dangerous characteristic. Chap. 3.

Super-incompetence—complete lack of output and input: grounds for dismissal. Chap. 3.

Super-incumbent—a person above you who, having reached his level of incompetence, blocks your path to promotion. Chap. 4.

Tabulatory gigantism—obsession with large-size desks. Chap. 12.

Tabulology, abnormal—the study of unusual arrangements of desks, workbenches, etc. Chap. 12.

Tabulophobia Privata—inability to tolerate the presence of desks. Chap. 12.

Teeter-Totter Syndrome—inability to make decisions. Chap. 12.

Temporary relief—results of medical treatment for Final Placement Syndrome. Chap. 11.

Universal hierarchiology—an untapped field of study. Chap. 7.

Utter Irrelevance—a Substitution technique common at upper levels of commerce. Chap. 13.

A Note on the Illustrations

The authors and the publishers of *The Peter Principle*
appreciate the special permission granted by the Managing
Director of *Punch* to reproduce the drawings without the
original captions. For anyone who might be interested, in
addition to the name of the artist and the year of publication, we are providing as follows the complete text that
accompanied each illustration when it first appeared:

Page 10   Charles Keene (1888)

REPRISALS!

*Tradesman (to Old Gentleman, who has purchased Lawn-
Mower).* "Yes, sir, I'll oil it, and send it over imm—"
Customer (imperatively). No, no, no!—It mustn't be oiled!
I won't have it oiled! Mind that! I want noise! And, look here—
pick me out a nice rusty one. My neighbour's children hoot and
yell till ten o'clock every night, so"—(*viciously*)—"I mean to
cut my grass from four till six every morning!!"

Page 15   G. du Maurier (1889)

AN AWKWARD REPARTEE TO DEAL WITH.

Head Master. "It's disgraceful, sir! Why, your brother, who
is two years younger than yourself, knows his Greek grammar
better than you do!"
Dunce. "Ah, but my brother's not been here so long as I
have, sir. It's only his first term!"

Page 21   G. du Maurier (1889)

TROP DE ZÈLE.

Clerical Customer. "I want to buy a nice diamond brooch for my better half."

Over-anxious Shopkeeper. "Certainly, sir. We have just the very thing. We can accommodate you also for your other half, if you wish."   [*They did not trade.*

Page 26   Charles Keene (1864)

AN EXCELLENT EXCUSE.

This is Jack Sparkles, who used to be such a thorough preraphaelite, as we came upon him "at work" the other day—at least he called it so. He said he had come to the conclusion that "painting was, after all, more or less a matter of memory, and that he was studying skies!!"

Page 31   W. Ralston (1871)

PRACTICAL.

Fond Father. "I see ye've put my son intil graummer an' jography. Noo, as I neither mean him tae be a minister or a sea-captain, it's o' nae use. Gie him a plain bizness eddication."

Page 34   G. du Maurier (1887)

A DAY IN THE COUNTRY.

Little Tommy (who has never been out of Whitechapel before). "Oh! Oh! Oh!"

Kind Lady. "What's the matter, Tommy?"

Little Tommy. "Why, what a big sky they've got 'ere, Miss!"

Page 47   Charles Keene (1874)

VERY MUCH CARED FOR.

Chorus of Ladies (to comely Curate). "O, Mr. Sweetlow, do take care! Don't go up!—So dangerous! Do come down! O!"

Rector (sarcastically). "Really, Sweetlow, don't you think you'd better let a married man do that?!!"

Page 55   Charles Keene (1886)

A PESSIMIST.

Exemplary Clerk. "Can I have a week's holiday, if you please, sir? A—a domestic affliction, sir—"

Employer. "Oh, certainly, yes, Mr. —— Dear me, I'm very sorry! 'Near relative?"

Clerk. "Ah—ye'—n'—that is—you misunderst— What I mean, sir—I'm going to be married!"

Page 67   A. C. Corbould (1885)

LIKE HIS CHEEK.

" 'Old yer 'oss, sir?"

Page 73   E. T. Reed (1892)

ELECTION INTELLIGENCE.

Brilliant Elector (at the Polling Station). "It's a stoutish koind of a man, with a bald 'ead, as ar wishes to vote for, but ar'm blessed if ar know 'is naame!!"

Page 86   W. T. Maud (1891)

IT'S A GREAT THING FOR A MAN TO KNOW WHEN HE'S WELL OFF.

Page 93   G. du Maurier (1883)

A FAIR RETORT.

Mrs. Mountjoy Belassis (after several Collisions). "It strikes me, Mr. Rudderford, you're much more at home in a boat than in a ball-room!"

Little Bobby Rudderford (the famous Oxbridge Coxswain). "Yes, by Jove! And I'd sooner steer eight men than one woman *any* day!"

Page 105   Charles Keene (1874)

SHOCKING!

Dr. Jolliboy (who had been called away from a social Meeting at his Club). "Thirteen, fourteen, f'fteen-two, f'fteen-four, f'fteen-six—pair eight—nob'sh nine——" *(Drops off.)*

["*We draw a Veil,*" &c., &c.

Page 114   John Leech (1862)

OLD SCHOOL.

Mr. Grapes (helping himself to another glass of that fine old Madeira). "Hah! We live in strange times—what the dooce can people want with drinking fountains!"

Page 122   E. T. Reed (1891)

DRAWING THE LINE.

Judge. "Remove those barristers. They're drawing!"
Chorus of Juniors. "May it please your Ludship, we're only drawing—pleadings."

Page 136   A. C. Corbould (1885)

"RUS IN URBE."

Fair Equestrian (from the Provinces, her first turn in the Row). "Good gracious, Sam! You can't ride out with me like that! Where are your boots and things?"
Country Groom. "Lor', Mum, I didn't bring 'em up. But it don't matter. Nobody knows me here!"

Page 143   Charles Keene (1880)

DEFINITIVE.

Board Schoolmaster (desiring to explain the word "Conceited," which had occurred in the course of the Reading Les-

son). "Now, Boys, suppose that I was always boasting of my Learning—that I knew a good deal o' Latin for instance, or that my personal appearance was—that I was very Good-looking, y' know—what should you say I was?"

Straightforward Boy (*who had "caught the Speaker's eye"*). "I sh' say you was a Liar, S'!"

Page 147   G. du Maurier (1890)

STUDIES IN REPARTEE.

She. "How silent you are! What are you thinking of?"
He. "Nothing!"
She. "Egotist!"

Page 158   G. du Maurier (1882)

A GOOD-BYE TO JOLLY WHITBY.

The Browns and their Family drag their Luncheon-Baskets over the Dam on the Esk for the last time, alas! And for the last time, Brown Senior attempts a feeble French Joke, beginning "Esker la Dam——" and, as usual, falls down on the slippery Stones before he can finish it!

Page 168   G. du Maurier (1882)

"NOT FOND OF STEERING? JUST AIN'T WE THOUGH!"

A Note About the Authors

Laurence J. Peter was born in Canada and received an Ed.D. from Washington State University. With wide experience as a teacher, counselor, school psychologist, prison instructor, consultant, and university professor, he has written more than thirty articles that have appeared in professional journals, and a book, *Prescriptive Teaching* (1965). He is now Associate Professor of Education, Director of the Evelyn Frieden Center for Prescriptive Teaching, and Coordinator of Programs for Emotionally Disturbed Children at the University of Southern California.

Raymond Hull, the son of an English Methodist minister, has lived in British Columbia since 1947. He has had thirty TV and stage plays produced and four stage plays published. His articles have been featured in such magazines as *Punch, Macleans* and *Esquire*.